FORGING A NATION

Written by,
Linda Zimmermann
with,
Richard F. Ricca

Eagle Press
New York

Also by Linda Zimmermann

Bad Astronomy

Forging A Nation

Copyright 1996 by Linda Zimmermann.

ISBN:0-9645133-1-5

In memory of my father,

Walter J. Zimmermann

A man who proudly served the country he loved.

United States Marine Corps
1st Marine Division
WWII
Korea

Acknowledgments

One of the best parts of writing this book was coming into contact with all the fascinating people who have devoted their time to the preservation of our country's history. I am deeply grateful for their enthusiasm, expertise and willingness to share their knowledge.

Alan Aimone, United States Military Academy Library, West Point, New York.
Robert Brennan, Sackets Harbor, New York.
Lori Childers, Knox's Headquarters, Vails Gate, New York.
Brian Leigh Dunnigan, Old Fort Niagara, New York.
Diane Kurtz, Bridgeport Public Library, Bridgeport, Connecticut.
Douglas Reed Niermeyer, Beacon, New York.
Phil Porter, Mackinac State Historic Parks, Mackinac Island, Michigan.
Walter Powell, Gettysburg National Historic Park, Gettysburg, Pennsylvania.
The staff of the United States Military History Institute, Carlisle Barracks, Pennsylvania.
&
The staff and volunteers of Historic Societies and libraries across the country.

Also, special thanks to my brother, Jim, for the computer, to Susan Sciotto-Brown for her encouragement and technical support, to Steven Harnish for the camera equipment and to Robert A. Strong for the maps, the "field trips" and for putting up with me.

Introduction by Richard Ricca

During the time *Forging A Nation* was being written, many people asked the same questions: How did I acquire over 500 documents, letters and diaries pertaining to the same military family from the 1790's to the 20th century? Did it take many years of painstaking research, working with various military institutions and resource centers throughout the country? Why did I chose the Thompson family? Was I related to them? How did I know where to go to get a book written?

The truth of the matter is simply that the documents *"found me"*, and I was extremely lucky to find Linda Zimmermann. The way this book developed restored my faith in fate. I simply purchased an old trunk that I glanced at from 15 feet away, in an upstate New York antique shop. Neither I nor the dealer took the time to explore the contents. Two weeks later, after driving thousands of miles with the trunk wedged in the back seat of my car, I finally went through the contents and was completely amazed to find all of the Thompsons' papers. This took place in 1993, exactly two hundred years from the signing of the earliest document in the trunk.

I immediately looked into putting these documents into book form, to share with my fellow Military Historians, with whom I have been proud to associate for the past 25 years, but I became frustrated not knowing how to accomplish it. Then one day unexpectedly, Linda Zimmermann called me (not knowing of the Thompson documents) to ask about some information for an article she was writing on Civil War reenactments. Nonchalantly, I brought up the documents and we discussed the possibility of "teaming up" for the purpose of publishing the collection in a chronological, as well as a reader-friendly, manner. Six months later, the idea began to become a reality.

I thank God Linda has a lot of will power and spirit. She has worked literally night and day, seven days a week, thinking, talking and dreaming about the Thompson documents. She has traveled thousands of miles and called dozens of people throughout the country to research the names, places and events mentioned in the hundreds of letters and documents from that old trunk.

I know this book would not be in your hands now if it hadn't been for the total commitment of Linda Zimmermann.

Richard F. Ricca
Nanuet, New York

Mr. Ricca will donate ten percent of the proceeds from this book to St. Ann's Church, Nyack, New York.

Author's Note

Shortly after beginning this project, I realized that I could write a book about writing this book. While every day brought some new discovery, I would like to briefly describe two of the particularly special days to illustrate what I mean.

Early one spring morning, I went to the United States Military Academy Library at West Point, New York. I thought I would spend an hour going over a few books and documents. Almost six hours later, I finally tore myself away from the library's incredible collection. However, despite being tired and hungry, I had found some information which indicated that at least one of the Thompsons was buried somewhere in the cemetery and I couldn't leave without taking a look.

It was a dreary, rainy afternoon and as I pulled into the cemetery, I realized that it could take hours to search the vast rows of markers and monuments. Undaunted, I decided to test my luck. Less than five minutes later, I was standing amidst the Thompsons; between father and son, mother and daughter, husband and wife. A project which had begun as an interesting, academic pursuit, suddenly became much more.

At that moment, the Thompsons ceased being just signatures on old papers; they were living, breathing, feeling people who fell in love, struggled to raise their families and had hopes and dreams for the future. At that moment, I felt as if these people who I had been studying for so long, were members of my own family and I now had the responsibility, and privilege, of bringing their stories to light.

As the months passed and the manuscript neared completion, I knew something was missing; I wanted to see the faces of Captain Thompson and his son, Colonel Thompson. I had almost given up hope of ever finding any pictures of them, until one steamy August day when I went to Knox's Headquarters in Vails Gate, New York, to do some research. When I arrived, I found that an artillery reenactment group was there; Colonel John Lamb's Artillery, which Captain Thompson had joined during the Revolutionary War! After telling the men about my project, they braved the brutal heat and humidity and kindly put on their wool uniform coats so that I could photograph them.

A few minutes later, I struck up a conversation with another spectator, Douglas Reed Niermeyer, who happened to be a member of the Sons of the American Revolution and The Society of the Cincinnati. I told him about the book and he offered to try to track down any living Thompsons. By the time I got home that evening, there was already a message from Mr. Niermeyer saying that he had located two living Thompsons and they possessed portraits of the Captain and the Colonel!

After having become so completely absorbed with all the Thompsons who were long gone, it was strangely exciting to speak with Mr. Alexander R. Thompson and his brother, Mr. Robert S. Thompson; something like picking up the phone, asking to speak to George Washington and getting a response. Both men were extremely interested and helpful and most importantly, they were kind enough to share those portraits with me, so that I could finally look into the faces of my "old friends".

I received the sad and surprising news of the death of Mr. Alexander R. Thompson
the week I completed the manuscript.

Linda Zimmermann

THOMPSON FAMILY TREE

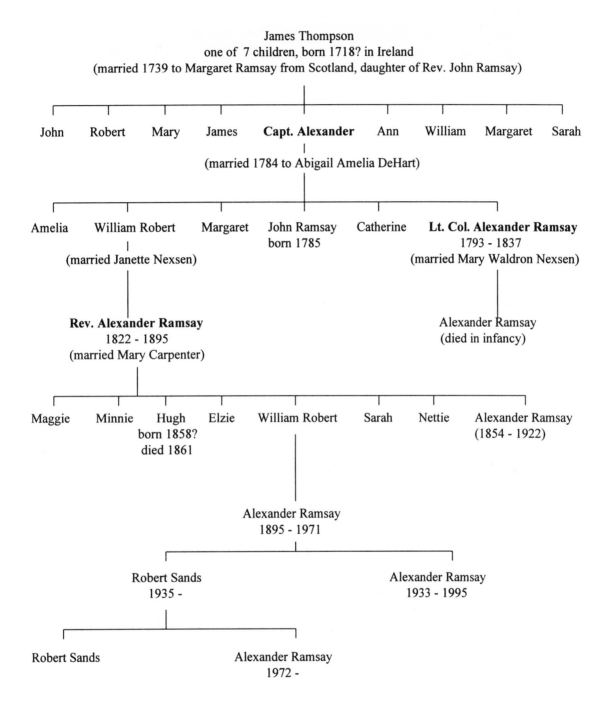

James Thompson
one of 7 children, born 1718? in Ireland
(married 1739 to Margaret Ramsay from Scotland, daughter of Rev. John Ramsay)

John   Robert   Mary   James   **Capt. Alexander**   Ann   William   Margaret   Sarah

(married 1784 to Abigail Amelia DeHart)

Amelia   William Robert   Margaret   John Ramsay   Catherine   **Lt. Col. Alexander Ramsay**
born 1785   1793 - 1837
(married Janette Nexsen)   (married Mary Waldron Nexsen)

Rev. Alexander Ramsay   Alexander Ramsay
1822 - 1895   (died in infancy)
(married Mary Carpenter)

Maggie   Minnie   Hugh   Elzie   William Robert   Sarah   Nettie   Alexander Ramsay
born 1858?   (1854 - 1922)
died 1861

Alexander Ramsay
1895 - 1971

Robert Sands   Alexander Ramsay
1935 -   1933 - 1995

Robert Sands   Alexander Ramsay
1972 -

Table of Contents

The transcriptions of the documents (*in italics*) throughout
the text have been copied verbatim, including the numerous
errors in grammar, spelling and punctuation.

Chapter 1

"This Young and Growing Country"

Captain Alexander Thompson, 1759-1809. (Courtesy of Thompson family.)

History is not a straight chain of dates, events and places. It is an intricately woven tapestry of people's lives and it is impossible to isolate a single thread of the fabric without losing the rich textures and colors which make the picture intriguing. Every individual is an indispensable part of that picture and the study of one person inevitably leads to ever-widening circles of men and women whose struggles and triumphs intertwine to give us a fascinating view of the past.

The Thompson Documents in the Ricca Collection represent a window into that past and show a picture of the United States framed by the words of three generations of an American family spanning the birth of our country to its rebirth as an inseparable union. The first-hand accounts contained in this collection offer a unique opportunity to view history from a personal perspective, to experience it in a manner which not only challenges the mind, but often touches the heart.

From these letters it becomes evident that the United States of America is not the product of clever generals and ambitious politicians. This nation is the result of the combined efforts of generations of common people thrust into the all-too-common occurrence of war. Our country began in war, was torn apart and redefined in war and right or wrong, we have taken up arms around the world in the name of our national ideals.

The men who fought in these wars were not nameless ranks of soldiers, they were fathers, brothers, husbands and sons. Some gained fame from their actions, but most simply did their duty and if they were lucky, quietly returned home to their families to enjoy a hard-won peace. Unfortunately, war does not discriminate and the families of these soldiers were often swept into, or swept away by, the conflicts. Women not only had to take over the duties of their absent men, but they and their children were frequently innocent victims of colliding armies. Despite this seeming penchant for self-destruction, however, we somehow managed to survive as families, states and a nation.

One such family which survived was that of Alexander Thompson of New York. Thompson and his descendants played a role in much of the turmoil in the 18th and 19th centuries. While none attained the highest ranks or widespread popularity, each faithfully served his country and by his efforts and sacrifices, helped forge this nation into what it is today.

Courtesy of Thompson Family.
Thompson family coat of arms. Their
motto was, "While I breathe I hope."

Captain Alexander Thompson[1] was born in New York City on August 17, 1759. His father, James, was most likely born and raised in Ballymena in Northern Ireland and moved to America as a young man. James Thompson married Margaret Ramsay, the daughter of a Scottish Presbyterian clergyman and together they had nine children, the youngest of them being Alexander. At the start of the Revolutionary War, Alexander's brothers, James and William, were successful businessmen who were imprisoned by the British in the Old Sugar House on Liberty Street and had all of their goods and money confiscated[2]. Apparently, the brothers would have starved in prison were it not for the aid of their neighbors, the family of Washington Irving[3].

After such treatment at the hands of the British, it is not surprising that the women of the Thompson family fled British-occupied New York. Unable to take baggage, they put on all the clothing they could wear and went to Madison, New Jersey; then known as Bottle Hill. The five brothers, John, Robert, James, William and Alexander, all took up arms against the British, with Alexander volunteering at the tender age of seventeen on February 7, 1777, in a company commanded by Captain Silvanus Seely.

---

[1] There have been at least nine Alexander Thompsons, including two still living.
[2] The information about Captain Thompson's parents and brothers is contained in letters and documents in the possession of the Thompson family. All other references are from the Ricca Collection, unless otherwise noted.
[3] Irving, author of such works as "Rip Van Winkle" and "The Legend of Sleepy Hollow", was born in 1783.

Official army records indicate that Alexander Thompson joined the Continental Army on May 31, 1779, as a lieutenant in the artillery. His commander was Colonel John Lamb, who had been with Benedict Arnold during the ill-fated attack of Quebec and was wounded[4] during the battle. Thompson served with Lamb's artillery until June of 1783, when he came under the command of Colonel John Crane. While some of Thompson's schooling in artillery may have taken place at Pluckemin, New Jersey, a training facility used during the summer of 1779, the first record of Thompson's location is in September of that year at Chester, New York, a small town about fifteen miles west of West Point. While there are no documents in the collection tracking his moves during the war, Thompson was definitely "present at the capture of Yorktown and other successes"[5].

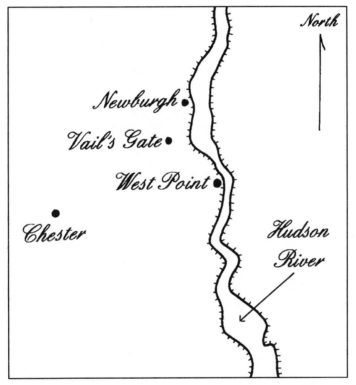

Robert A. Strong

At the end of the war, Thompson was "sent by the Commander in Chief with dispatches to the British frontier posts to announce the close of hostilities."[6] Such a mission could not have been an easy one; travel was hard business and the untamed wilds of late 18th century America were full of hostile elements and treacherous conditions. It

---

[4] Lamb's left cheekbone was shattered and he lost an eye. Captured by the British, Lamb was not released until January, 1777 when he returned to the Continental Artillery.
[5] Inscription on Thompson's grave marker at West Point, NY.
[6] Ibid.

is interesting to note that such perilous duty was to be taken up by his son, Lt. Col. Alexander Ramsay Thompson, who also had to endure the rigors of service along the frontier and would bravely pay the ultimate price in the Battle of Okeechobee in Florida. Such a life was difficult enough for the soldier, but arguably it could be even worse for the wives and families who either went for years without seeing their loved one or were constantly being uprooted and sent to remote locations where the only signs of civilization were within the relatively tenuous walls of the local fort.

There is a gap in the records[7] during the period immediately following the war until October 4, 1786, when Thompson was appointed to the rank of Captain in the New York Militia's Regiment of Artillery, commanded by Lt. Col. Sebastian Bauman. Then for the next seven years, there are no letters or documents, which naturally raises the question as to what Thompson was doing during that period. A letter from Joseph Howell at the War Department dated March 4, 1793, offers evidence that Thompson remained in service of the United States for at least a portion of those seven years.

"The Secretary of War having authorized you to muster your recruits and directed duplicate rolls to be transmitted to his Office, I shall cause pay rolls to be made agreeably thereto the amount of which will be remitted to you through the Supervisor of the Revenue for the district of New York..."

This kind of correspondence (accounts, muster rolls and duplicate receipts for everything) would fill the remainder of Thompson's life. While they may not make interesting reading, they provide valuable information about the early days of the new government. Unfortunately, the average person knows little about the period between the Revolutionary and Civil Wars, but it was during these crucial years that our infant nation gained its footing and began to expand. In a letter dated April 11, 1795, Thompson refers to the United States as *"this young and growing country"* and expresses his optimism for the future.

---

[7] The lack of documents from this period may be explained by the fact that Captain Thompson's grandson, Reverend Alexander Ramsay Thompson, lost his house in a fire in 1856; a fire which claimed the family Bible and probably many other important family papers.

The future for Thompson was mostly to be spent in military service. On June 2, 1794, he was promoted by President George Washington to Captain of the newly created Corps of Artillerists and Engineers. He wrote of this promotion to Major General Henry

Secretary of War Henry Knox's signature from the War Department.

This house in Vails Gate, New York was used as a headquarters
by General Knox during the Revolutionary War.

Knox, the first Secretary of War of the United States. Knox, a bookseller before the war, became one of George Washington's most valued officers. In addition to being in charge of the Continental Artillery, Knox played a key role in the crossing of the Delaware[8],

---

[8] A major contribution Knox made at the crossing was inadvertent. Demoralized by biting cold and wet uniforms, the men were cheered by General George Washington, at the expense of Knox's wide girth. After entering the boat, Washington declared to Knox, "Shift that fat ass, Harry - but slowly, or you'll swamp the *#!@! boat." The comment, quickly followed by laughter, raced down the lines of men and in the words of author Howard Fast, "Henry Knox's buttocks became the symbol of the moment."

engaged in battles at Brandywine, Germantown, Monmouth and Yorktown and accepted the surrender of the British in New York. The following letter indicates that it was Knox who personally informed Thompson of his promotion.

New York June 6, 1794

Sir

Yesterday I had the honor to receive by the hand of Colonel Bauman your notice of the 4th Instant in which you are pleased to inform me that the President of the United States has appointed me a Captain in the Corps of Artillerists and Engineers. I beg leave most respectfully to express my acceptance and that I have the honor to be with great respect and esteem Sir,

Your Most Obedient and very Humble Servant

Alex. Thompson

Thompson family.

Thompson's commission to the Corps of Artillerists and Engineers signed

by President George Washington and Secretary of War Henry Knox.

The Corps of Artillerists and Engineers was formed after an act of Congress on May 9, 1794. The commander of the Corps was Lieutenant Colonel Stephen Rochefontaine, a former officer in the French Royal Corps of Engineers. Like so many of his countrymen, Rochefontaine was stirred by the American cause and came to the

United States to offer his services to General Washington. Arriving in May of 1778, by September he was a Captain in the Continental Army and went on to earn the rank of Major for his efforts at the Battle of Yorktown.

Once peace had been made with the British, Rochefontaine decided to return to his native country. However, life was not quiet in late 18th century France. The flame of American freedom had sparked a fire among the French citizenry. The resulting heat apparently became too much for Rochefontaine and after Louis the XVI was beheaded on January 21, 1793, the Major fled to the United States. Fortunately, France's loss was to become our gain as the skilled Rochefontaine brought his valuable knowledge to the new Corps of Artillerists and Engineers.

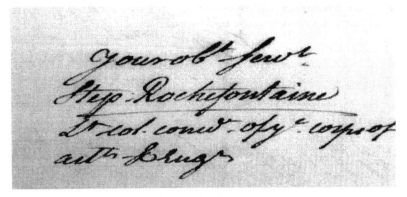

Signature of Lt. Col. Stephen Rochefontaine.

Rochefontaine recognized that despite our victory against the British, our armed forces lacked the training and education that European military schools provided. Washington and Knox had also both expressed the desire for an American academy to instruct soldiers of the future. The vision of these men started to come into focus when Rochefontaine began a school, with a few books written in French and very little equipment, at the small town on the Hudson River where the Corps was stationed, West Point, New York. Unfortunately, after only a year in operation the school burned down in 1796, but the seed had been planted.

Second in command of the Corps was another Frenchman, Colonel Louis de Tousard. Tousard, like Rochefontaine, fought with the Continental Army. During a battle in Rhode Island, Tousard lost an arm and was granted a pension for life by Congress, but still continued to serve his new country even after the war. Ironically, although both of

Signature of Colonel Louis de Tousard.

these officers served with distinction, this French connection so valuable to our struggle for freedom, was to become a slight embarrassment in the ensuing years when deteriorating relations with the Revolutionary French government highlighted our dependence on the French and accentuated the need for American self-reliance

While the commanders for the new Corps were stationed at West Point, Thompson began his career as Captain on Governor's Island off the southern tip of Manhattan. At this point in the thirty-five-year-old Captain's life, he had a wife, Amelia DeHart[9], a nine-year-old son, John Ramsay, another son, William Robert[10] (date of birth unknown), a four-year-old daughter, Amelia, and the one-year-old son who would follow in so many of his father's footsteps, Alexander Ramsay Thompson. There would be two more daughters, Margaret and Catherine, born in 1796 and 1799, as well as two other children who, Thompson poignantly related, died in infancy. The pay received from his promotion must have been no small comfort to Captain Thompson and his young and growing family.

What wasn't comforting was Governor's Island in 1794. The island had seen a military presence from the Dutch and British for over 150 years, but the new corps was not to have the benefit of any fine European architecture. When they arrived in August, tents provided their only shelter and the lack of clothing and blankets was not a problem in the New York heat. However, as the months passed and temperatures dropped, their situation changed dramatically. Thompson's compassion and concern for his men are clearly evident in the following excerpts.

To Joseph Howell, War Department:

Governor's Island Sept. 1: 1794-
...permit me to assure you they are good men, most of whom for years I have personally known. And that it is extremely painful for me, that no provision has been made to clothe them...

---

[9] A DAR Patriot Index lists her name as Abigail Amelia de Hart, but no other records, including her grave marker, use the name Abigail. Alexander Thompson and Amelia de Hart were married in Morristown, New Jersey on March 4, 1784.
[10] The father of Reverend Alexander Ramsay Thompson.

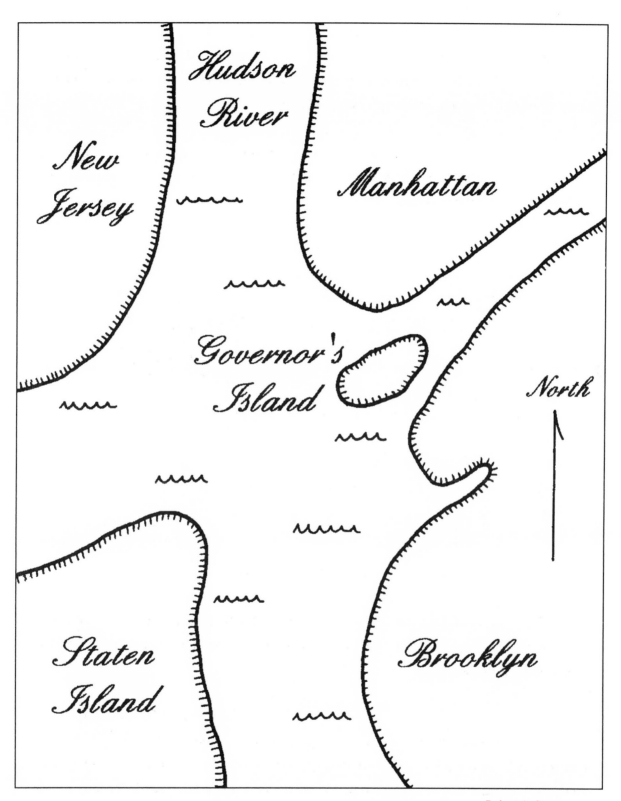

New Jersey

Hudson River

Manhattan

Governor's Island

North

Staten Island

Brooklyn

Robert A. Strong

11

To Knox:

Sir   *Governor's Island Nov. 8th: 1794-*
...will you be pleased to direct Mr. Hodgson to forward on some more suits of Clothing as the men Suffer extremely for want of them...

Sir   *Governor's Island Nov. 18th, 1794*
... No more clothing has arrived the men Suffer much at this season - and exposed situation on this Island...

Letter addressed to Captain Thompson from General Knox.

Finally, after four months of Thompson's attempts to get nothing more than clothing for his men, the following letter was sent by Samuel Hodgson at the War Department in Philadelphia:

Sir-   *Philadelphia 19th Nov 1794*
Yesterday the articles of Clothing mentioned in the enclosed invoice left this City for York - as the whole is immediately to your address I send this forward by Post to enable you to make enquiry should any unreasonable delay in forwarding them to you be attempted...

It appears that the only unreasonable delay in this matter was from the War Department. A week later, not only were Captain Thompson's men warmer, but Thompson also had *"the pleasure to forward"* to his friend Lt. McClallen in Albany *"ten compleat Suits of Clothing"* which *"Should have been immediately answered had it been in my power to do so."* And it would not be until December 11 that Thompson could report to Knox that finally the *"last twenty men under my command left their tents and took possession of one of the rooms in the brick barracks."*

It may seem odd that only ten years after the Revolution, soldiers stationed on an island to which city-dwellers would come for Sunday picnics, should be in such a sorry state. How could a country so proud of its Valley Forge and Jockey Hollow not rally to the aid of its former heroes?

The post-war attitudes toward the army had rapidly gone from admiration to suspicion; after all, it was the British standing army which had caused all the problems to begin with. Was the new federal government just going to pick up where the British had left off? A combination of public opinion and economic realities had effectively eliminated the navy and severely down-sized the army in the decade following the war. A military presence only minutes from Manhattan became a heated issue with New York politicians and citizens felt as if their new government didn't trust them.

Whatever optimism the young Captain had brought to his new command must have been sorely tested. Not only did Thompson have to deal with a government slow to respond to the basic needs of its soldiers, but also with a city that never missed an opportunity of showing its disrespect, or outright contempt to the military. In a letter to Alexander Hamilton, Thompson laments that the flag was not flown when his company was on the island and some of the city's *"Commissioners exclaimed publicly how shameful for troops of the United States to garrison Governors Island"*.

Such verbal disrespect was to be the least of Thompson's problems. On one occasion, he had to write to Mayor Richard Varick asking for his assistance in bringing to justice the townspeople who had beaten one of his soldiers. It is clear in the following letter to a Lt. Hutchins in Elizabethtown, New Jersey, that the problem was not isolated and it was serious, not only with civilians, but with new recruits as well.

Sir   *Governor's Island September 10th: 1794*
This afternoon your letter of yesterday is as delivered me by Mr. Cudworth. I am sorry you are under the Necessity of placing your recruits in Irons. As to want of small arms - I am just as you are, (not being furnished) but from the late riotous behaviour of some of the laborers on the fortifications I have armed my Men with

Muskets left in Store from Capt. Sedams detachment and am under the Necessity of Guarding the Magazine, with that of Camp Guards, no possible detachment can be admitted to take charge of your recruits - You had better direct a Warrant to the Goaler in Elizabeth Town or Newark and request him to take charge of & Safely keep - the Several persons (prisoners) belonging to the corps of Artillerists & Engineers - in the Service of the United States under your command.

Be pleased to accept my thanks for your very friendly enquiry of the health of my family.

Deserters

New recruits did not always join the army for patriotic reasons. For some, merely to get new clothes and three meals a day was incentive enough. Others were more devious; after collecting a bounty for signing-up, some recruits disappeared with cash and clothing.

Thompson on Governor's Island to McClallen in Albany, Dec. 29,1794:

...James Pratt has just deserted from this Island, and that like a bad man has taken the whole of compleat suit of clothing with him, as it is possible he will make for that part of the country from which he came, I have to request you will exert yourself to have him apprehended and properly secured until opportunity will offer to send him to me -

The problem was one of surprising proportions. A muster roll of Fort Niagara from April of 1799 shows that out of 38 officers and men, 17 had deserted at some point. This astounding 45% desertion rate may be explained in part by the poor living conditions to which soldiers were often subjected, as well as the harsh punishments meted out by many officers. Civil prisons in the 18th century were generally temporary holding cells where the convicted waited a few days until the sentence of corporal punishment could be inflicted; military justice was no different. Below is an example of one harsh form of punishment (which could have had dangerous consequences) and then the explanation as to why it was deemed necessary.

Unsigned, most likely written from Governor's Island March 29, 1796:

Sir This is to inform your Honor that Stephen Brant was whipt the 25th and Received thirty two Lashes without the Benefit of a Court Martial and one Kelly at the Same time Belonging to Captain Gambels Company and the Said Kelly has Deserted Since and one Lupton Belonging to Captain Wadsworths Company, and those two there is Nothing

---

heard of them Since - The men in all have been very much Dissatisfied With Lieut. Geddes and I believe <u>if there is any more Floged I believe it will turn to Mutiny</u> -

To Thompson at West Point from (Trau?) on Governor's Island, March 31, 1799:

Sir

  As Lieut. Geddes mode of Government has given General uneasiness in this Garrison and understanding that You were Dissatisfied with it so far as it suspected Day & Brant and Lieunt. Geddes fearing that you would have a misinterpretation of the matter Would beg to lay before you a Candid & impartial Statement of the facts as Crimes for which they were punished -

  It seems that they had agreed to leave the Island together for Day being in Town as an Oars-man Deserted from us after it was Dark & Could not be found Brant the same night after tattoo by some Stratagem left the Island & went to Town where they Lodged together Day returned before it was light Brant continued there till sent for the next Day about ten O'Clock - Notwithstanding they were Generously pardoned by Lieut. Geddes -

  The next night they left the Island again after tattoo, Day returning as before, Brant continued till sent for -

  Day for the last offense was sentenced to mount Guard which he refused to Do, <u>therefore was punished with stripes</u> - Whether Such Crimes ought to be punished with stripes or Whether Lieut. Geddes ought to inflict stripes is not for me to Determine, but be Assured Sir I am not a friend to Arbitrary Government...

  To aid in apprehending deserters, a detailed description of physical characteristics and appearance accompanied the new recruits when being sent to their posts. Their place of birth and former residence is also listed, possibly to give a clue as to where absentee soldiers might be headed.

  Lt. Horatio Dayton in Elizabeth Town to Thompson on Governor's Island, June 6, 1794:

  1. Thomas Codee 24 years old 5 feet 6 inches high, an Irishman lived at Morris Town New Jersey, Labourer, brown hair, grey eyes, fair complexion - Thomas Codee has drawn his Clothing complete except 2 pair shoes Inlisted 22nd: Dec. 1794 -
  2. Henry Bryan 21 years old 5 feet 10 inches high, born in Derry Ireland, Labourer, Brown hair, blue eyes, Fresh complexion, inlisted 18th: May 1794 2 Linen Overalls, 1 pair Shoes
  3. Samuel Caton 27 years old 5. 9 1/2 inches high born at Hartford, Wheelright...
  4. James Marey 20 years old, 5. 6 1/2 inches high, Ireland...
  5. John Dyckman 45 years old, 5. 8 1/2 inches high, Harlem New York...
  6. John Lindiff 41 years of age, 5. 6 1/2 inches high, born in England...

As muster rolls show, many deserters were apprehended and actually returned to active duty (indicating just how desperate the army was for soldiers). While most were probably caught, punished and reinstated, in at least one case it appears as if a deserter attempted to escape punishment with a creative excuse for his prolonged absence.

Thompson's note on muster roll regarding Caleb Hoffman, Fort Niagara, April 1799:

Says he was taken by the Indians 24 August 1794.

There were also some men who risked punishment and deserted for rather compelling reasons.

From Thompson on Governor's Island to Major Pratt in Middle Town Connecticut, September 9, 1794:

Sir
David Taylor Drummer in Capt. Sedams company 1:Sub Legion, having absented himself from the Garrison it is to be Supposed he has made his way for Middle Town...On Taylors return from Capt. Sedams detachment in Jersey, Some recruits from West Point on this Island, on their way to Jersey, informed Taylor, that a Sergeant Munson of Middle Town had his Wife in Keeping...

Congress had authorized the building of fortifications on Governor's Island and day laborers from the city were employed to accomplish this goal. The *"riotous behavior"* about which Thompson wrote was the result of these unskilled men who didn't recognize the army's authority and seemed more often than not, to have been in varying degrees of intoxication. Drunkenness was no small problem, both with the day laborers and soldiers, who often found themselves court-martialed for their offenses.

At Garrison Court Martial held at Governors Island by order of Capt. Alexander Thompson for the trial of such prisoners as may be brought before it. Capt. Morris Presiding: Lieut. Elmer, Lieut. Dayton members.
The Court being duly sworn proceeded to the trial of Daniel Miller Private, charged with drunkeness when on guard - prisoner pleads guilt. Cornelius Sullivan charged with being drunk and absent from Roll call on the evening of the 16th June and fighting in the guard house - the prisoner pleads guilty to the whole charge -
Nicholas Doyle charged with being drunk at Roll call - pleads guilty -
Thomas Everton charged with being drunk at Roll call - prisoner pleads guilty -
Anthony Robertson charged with being drunk and absent from Roll call - pleads guilty -

George Howser - charged with being drunk on guard - the prisoner pleads guilty-

The Court on due consideration do sentence above named Daniel Miller, Cornelius Sullivan and George Howser to Four Weeks hard labor on the public works on this Island - Nicholas Doyle and Thomas Everton to two weeks - Anthony Robertson to Ten Days hard labor on the same works -

The Court adjourned without a day -

Staats Morris

Capt. in the Corps of A & E Presid.

It is likely that Thompson's "*dear little family*", as he referred to them, was not living on Governor's Island during these rough times, but was safely lodged in New York City, perhaps with Thompson's brother, John, who, by the late 1790's at least, lived at 310 Broadway. John, nineteen years older than Alexander, was more like a father to his youngest brother, as well as to the other family members who resided with him. It would be to his brother's home that Captain Thompson would return after being released from the army in 1802. However, it would be a long and draining road from 1794 back to his "*native city*" eight years later.

One event which was to prove both emotionally and financially draining, was a lawsuit brought against Thompson by two of those infamous day laborers. William Fitzgerald and Gilbert Pell accused Captain Thompson and Corporal George McKinley of assault and battery and unlawful imprisonment. Thompson hired lawyer Robert Troup to defend him. Troup, a fellow veteran of the Revolution, was a key figure in politics of the day. As a staunch supporter and intimate friend of Alexander Hamilton, Troup was a leader of the federalist [11] cause.

Thompson also met with and corresponded to Alexander Hamilton, who was practicing law in New York City, and asked if he would enlist the aid of the Attorney General in his defense. There seems to have been some concern as to whether Thompson and his corporal would get a fair trial, occasioned no doubt, by the ill feelings the townspeople held for the army. The story unfolds in a detailed series of letters.

From Troup to Thompson, October 10, 1795:

Sir   I did not expect you would have left town after what passed between us without letting me see you - I wanted to take from you a particular statement of all the

---

[11] The Federalist Party led by Alexander Hamilton, advocated a strong, centralized government. Thomas Jefferson and the Democratic Party were directly opposed to federalist policies.

circumstances respecting the suits brought against you by William Fitzgerald and by Gilbert Pell and also respecting the suit brought against your soldier George McKinley by Gilbert Pell. I removed the suits from Mr. Mayor's Court into the Supreme Court in order that you might have a better chance for a fair trial - and it is now necessary that special leave should be filed and that I should put in pleas for you. When the facts stated in these pleas will depend in great measure upon your success in the suits - Let me have therefore without a moments lapse of time a particular statement of all the circumstances regarding the imprisonment of the several plaintiffs in the suits -you must begin with stating that you are an officer of such rank - in such regiment commanded by such an officer in the service of the United States - That by an officer of such rank you had command of the fort - and name the fort - and whether it was a fort garrisoned of the state of New York or of the United States...that it became necessary for you to prevent all persons from strolling or walking about or in the fort or garrison after certain hours - mentioning the hours particularly - That to this end it was necessary for you to give out a countersign - and order all persons to be apprehended after certain hours who were found walking about without the countersign - that the several plaintiffs were taken up in conveyance of these orders - that they were confined for a certain time - mentioning the time and place of confinement - and afterwards released - mentioning when their release took place - were the plaintiffs any way beaten - what was their behavior and why they were taken up and what treatment in particular did they receive from you or your soldiers. You cannot be too minute and particular in giving me information upon all these points and the more minute and particular you are the better - They are suits of a serious nature to you and you should not let one hour pass away after this letter reaches you without sitting down and answering in the fullest manner possible - If you are guilty of any neglect the United States will never reimburse you the damages that may be recovered - so that it behooves you to be very attentive to the advice I give you - On my part there shall be no neglect...I ought to have your answer in 8 or 10 days at farthest - Let me entreat you to be expeditious in writing to me - within that time

I am Sir,

Your humble Servant

Rob. Troup

From Troup to Thompson at West Point, October 12, 1795:

If you could spare time I would rather see you in person - If you cannot come let me know the readiest way of getting a letter to you in case I should want further information from you after your answers to this letter come to hand -

- The particulars also in mentioning the time when the plaintiffs were taken up-

Signature of Robert Troup.

Thompson's response of November 21, 1795 from West Point:

Dear Sir,

In my letter to you of the 20th of June last I mentioned two writs had been served from Mayors Court - Pell and Fitzgerald against me and the corporal of the guard Mckinley for assault, Battery, and false Imprisonment. I am apt to think that letter from the subject of your two must have been passed over - on the 22nd of the same month of June I wrote to the Secretary of War informing him of the suits and that I had employed you as my attorney. And that I not only conceived it a case of the greatest moment to be determined as to myself - but asked it in behalf of the officers in the service of the United States. Governor's Island was named by law to be fortified for the defense of the harbor and front of New York. And I believe no name has been given to the fort on it[12] - As to my commission I bear that of Captain in the Regiment of Artillerists and Engineers in the Service of the United States Commanded by Stephen Rochefontaine Lt. Col. Comm. And that by orders of the Secy. of War. With my company I took charge of the Magazine and Stores on Gov. Island the 7th Feby. last that I rec'd. the orders of the Gov. of the State of New York as Commanding the forts in the harbor. Agreeable to his proclamation, and from the numbers of persons employed to labour on the publick Fortifications on Gov. Island among whom a number of robberies and abuses were committed it became necessary for the safety of publick property that some order should be observed, and as the persons employed to labour were employed by the State, it became my duty to apply to the Gov. for advice and direction and by his approbation a Countersign was given out after gun firing nine o'Clock at night, when all intercourse by water without permission or the word should be guarded against. The Countersign was known to be given out on

---

[12] The fort was to be named Fort Jay.

the evening of 16 May and continued and all persons of decency could have it - Pell out of contempt to order - came to the Island at his own late hour, landed at the dock near the Magazine, was taken charge of by the Guard until reported to me (notwithstanding his threats and abuses to the Guard) when he was released. As to violence no other was offered him, then detained till reported, it being a short time, no other verbal report was made. Fitzgeralds name I never heard until named in the Suits - in doing this I conceived I was doing my duty. No civil officer resided on the Island, two hundred men of every character to meet with, but my duty was to observe order and quiet and nine o'Clock at night, to arrest abuses - the Gov. further directed me to prevent any boats whatever from passing to the Island on Sunday - Suits may be brought against me for this instance. Oblige me so much as to let Col. Hamilton see this letter. Post days here are Tuesdays and Fridays - I am sir your most Ob. Humble Servant,

Alex. Thompson Captain
Corps of Artillerists and Engineers

Obviously leaving nothing to chance, a week later Thompson wrote directly to Alexander Hamilton.

Sir   *West Point December 5th: 1795*

My Lieut. McClallen who is so obliging as to promise to hand this to you, I beg leave to acquaint you. That the two persons who were confined by the Guard at Gov. Island for not observing the police established for the Safety of the Publick Stores, the order and quiet of the Island after night - appear determined , if in their power, to ruin me. Possibly you may recollect Sir that I mentioned some thing of this case when in New York. I have stated to Col. Troup - as circumstantially as I could recollect and requested he would be pleased to show to you - I am aware that nothing will be wanting to distress me - the tri colored flag was not Suffered to fly on Gov. Island when my company was there, substantially some of the Commissioners exclaimed publickly how Shamefull for troops of the United States to Garrison Governors Island, all these, with unhappy prejudices presents me their victim - Sir I have done no more than my duty - And I should hold myself bound to do it again, was I again like circumstances. If you will be pleased Sir with the Attorney General of the district to interpose in my behalf I shall then have that protection a regular duty intitles me to -

With great respect and Esteem, I have the honor to be Sir
Your most Obedient and very humble Servant
Alex. Thompson Captain   Corps of Artillerists & Engineers

The outcome of the lawsuit? There is no further mention of the case in the documents for almost a year. Then on November 27, 1796, Thompson states in simple terms what must have been a dramatic event. In a letter to William Simmons at the War Department, he relates that the "*Suit was determined in my favor in April term last - when Colonel Hamilton so obligingly Supported my cause - and the plaintifs obliged to leave the State*". This was clearly a case where two lowlifes looking to make an easy buck picked the wrong victim. One can only imagine their reactions when the mighty Alexander Hamilton came to Thompson's aid. With Hamilton's influence and powers of persuasion, it wouldn't have been surprising if the plaintiffs had been obliged to leave the country.

Unfortunately, this would not be the end of the Captain's legal problems. Some mysterious financial difficulties were to plague him in the impoverished last years of his life, to the point where he appears to have narrowly escaped "*the horrors of prison*". But at least by the fall of 1795, the horrors of Governor's Island were behind him and he was now stationed at West Point, New York. It is interesting to note that the attitude of the citizens of New York City toward the army on Governor's Island would change drastically in the ensuing years. The threat of war with France made nervous city-dwellers rally to the army's aid; even the distinguished professors and students of Columbia University picked up shovels and volunteered to help fortify Governor's Island's defenses. It's too bad that respect only followed fear.

View of Manhattan from fortifications of Fort Jay on Governor's Island (circa early 1800's).

Present-day view of Manhattan from Governor's Island.

A Loveless Triangle

France aided America during the Revolutionary War for two basic reasons. Firstly, many Frenchmen were enchanted by the underdog's fight for freedom against a tyrant. Secondly, and easily most important, France hated England. If this had not been the case, Louis XVI wouldn't have parted with a single franc to help us. However, this loveless triangle would quickly come back to haunt us.

Thompson on Governor's Island to Secretary of War Henry Knox, June 20, 1794:

I think it necessary to inform you that the two British Ships of War under command of Captain Rodgers which lay near the Island yesterday afternoon made sail and passed the Narrows whither they came to anchor at Sandy Hook or proceeded immediately to Sea, I have not as yet been able to learn -

Thompson on Governor's Island to Governor Clinton in New York, May 24, 1795:

This morning about 7 o'Clock the french Sloop of War Favourite, Captain Fleury, Made Sail from her Station near this Island and passed the Narrows - whither She came to anchor at Sandy Hook, or proceeded to Sea, I am not competent to Say-

Why all the interest in a few ships? For starters, British and French sailors didn't mix. In New York in 1793, a bloody battle broke out in the streets when sailors from the two countries met. Reports from other harbor towns indicated that rampaging bands of drunken Frenchmen beat anyone who even looked British. Then there was the fact that the British had begun the nasty habits of seizing American merchant vessels containing supplies for the French, as well as boarding these ships at sea and kidnapping anyone they suspected of being former British citizens. These unfortunate men were then virtually enslaved and forced to work on British naval vessels in their fight against the French. Often, Americans who couldn't prove their citizenship were also taken. As we had no navy to defend our ships, and trade with British ports was lucrative, this outrageous behavior was not seriously challenged at first.

As far as the French were concerned, things were more complicated. At the start of the French Revolution, Americans rejoiced and felt great satisfaction in the belief that our noble struggle for freedom was an inspiration to other nations. Lafayette even presented the keys of the Bastille to George Washington. However, with each drop of the guillotine, enthusiasm for the French cause waned and it became increasingly evident that a position of neutrality should be maintained with the fledging government of France.

France didn't see it that way; hadn't they saved us from the British, and wasn't it only right that we should now return the favor? To rally Americans to their cause, the French sent Edmond Charles Edouard Genet, who preferred to simply be called Citizen Genet. Arrogant, ill-tempered and lacking in good judgment, Citizen Genet was just charming enough to draw throngs of adoring Americans wherever he went. Even Thomas Jefferson was taken in by the man and his cause.

Genet blithely ignored our policy of neutrality and went about outfitting ships with American supplies, and American sailors, to prey upon British (or their allies) shipping. The following letter is from Thompson *"To the Captain Commanding the french Privateer lying in the harbor of New York"*, informing him that he and the Spanish ship he had captured were violating the law.

Sir   *Governor's Island June 19th:1795*

By proclamation of His Excellency the Governor of the State of New York, No Vessel of War or privateer of any of the Belligerent powers, be permitted to pass or come to any station within one mile South of this Island, you will be pleased to observe this notice, and remove the Vessel under your command, accordingly-

The Captain, who appeared conveniently ignorant of the law, nonetheless requested permission to go to a harbor to refit his ship.

Sir   *East River 19 June 1795*

I have just now received the honour of yours of this day. Permit me to observe you that my privateeri has been fitted out at Port de Paix in hispaniola (Haiti) and have brought my prize in there, coming up by Sound and Hells' gate. I was quite ignorant of his Excellency's the governor's proclamation and as a friend to order and Laws of an allie-nation I am ready to comply with; I will nevertheless take Leave to add, that my vessel stands in need of being refitted and that the case is of a very pressing nature, whereupon I intend this very day and no farther to apply myself to his excellency's grace to get permission to lay in East river in order to receive such relief as my Condition may require.   accept of my respectful Sentiments of

Your most obedient Servant

S Berard

Captain of the privateeri Vengeance

of Port de Paix-

After American officials inspected the ship, it was indeed found to be in "*want of caulking*" and "*was permitted to pass into the east River*" for repairs. Thompson informed both Governor De Witt Clinton and Secretary of War Timothy Pickering of the situation, and continued to apprise both men (as well as Clinton's successor, Governor John Jay, sworn in July 3, 1795) of any French or British vessels spotted in waters around New York.

George Washington continually reasserted our neutral position and demanded an end to the practice of supporting French pirates. The outraged Genet declared that Washington was an old, incompetent fool who was jealous of the fact that Genet was more popular with the people and more influential with the government. Or so Genet thought. As Genet's antics and derogatory remarks came to be known, support for the diplomat crumbled, both in the United States and France. The French government was so dismayed that they sent orders for his arrest and immediate return to France; a request which no doubt would have led to the Citizen's head in a basket.

In a remarkable display of character, George Washington, the man most maligned by Genet, no doubt saved the Frenchman's life by allowing him to stay in the country. For once, Genet acted prudently. He dropped out of the public eye, managed to marry the daughter of New York's Governor Clinton and lived the quiet life of a country gentleman. Unfortunately, getting rid of Genet didn't get rid of the French (or British) problem.

By the end of 1797, French ships had seized over 300 American merchant vessels; insurance rates skyrocketed, commerce was suffocating and it was (undeclared) war. The army greatly increased its numbers and a tiny U.S. Navy was formed. However, despite these preparations for all-out war, there were only three confrontations at sea and the matter was resolved through diplomatic channels in 1800. Even though no lands were conquered, the revitalized economic situation allowed us to claim victory in the quasi-war with France. As for the British, it eventually became evident that mutual cooperation was far more prosperous than kidnapping.

Incidents such as these during the 1790's proved that reliance on foreign nations for training and expertise could be a dangerous thing. Americans had been pushed around long enough by their European big brothers and even though the army quickly shrank back to its pre-quasi-war size, the need for an American military academy with American instructors became clearly evident. The seed that Washington, Knox and Rochefontaine planted would soon sprout and bear some amazing fruit.

Based upon the few documents in the collection concerning West Point during this period, Thompson's years there appear to have been relatively quiet[13] . The first piece of correspondence which indicates his new residence was dated October 9, 1795 and indicates that Thompson was probably not alone on the move from Governor's Island to West Point, and probably not sorry to have left.

From Lt. Dayton, (the new) Commander of Governor's Island, to Thompson at West Point, October 9, 1795:

Sir

I am surprised I have not received a line from you before this time according to your promise, I expected to have had some men sent to me before this, the duty is very hard, the men are on guard every other day -

I expected likewise to have heard about money for recruiting, and about my getting to Philadelphia. All is well, fired a Salute on Sunday - had to do all the business myself for want of men.

Things necessarily had to be more quiet at West Point; in the late 1790's, there were no roads leading out of West Point to any major towns, leaving the river as the only viable route for supplies and communication. Yet, due to the geography of the area, it was no easy matter transporting supplies from the docks to the garrison. What made West Point's location on the heights above the Hudson River so valuable strategically, made it a nightmare, physically, for those who had to carry heavy equipment up the steep slopes; even cannons were hauled strictly by manpower. One solution to this problem was to build warehouses by the docks and then have supplies sent up only as needed.

Everything was carefully counted and recorded and the emphasis was clearly on economy, not comfort. An example of this can be found in a requisition[14] for flour dated May, 1796. What made this request unusual is that the flour was not to be used for baking bread; it was to be used as a replacement for the more costly white powder which men of the times put in their hair, according to the fashion of the day. One can only imagine the sticky results of standing guard in the rain or marching on a steamy, August afternoon with hair full of flour.

---

[13] The years 1795-1798. His return in 1802 until his death in 1809 were complicated with financial and legal problems and ill health.

[14] U.S. Military Academy Library at West Point, New York.

Northern Confederates?

Timothy Pickering was born in Salem, Massachusetts in 1745. He is credited with leading the first armed resistance (although no shots were fired) of Americans against the British on February 26, 1775. After fighting in the Revolutionary War at such battles as Brandywine and Germantown and holding the position of Quartermaster General, Pickering continued to serve his country as Postmaster General, Secretary of War and Secretary of State, as well as representing his home state of Massachusetts both as a Senator and a Congressman. With such credentials, one would think Timothy Pickering was the epitome of the American statesman.

As Commander of Governor's Island, Thompson exchanged correspondence with Secretary of War Pickering about supplies, recruits and arms and ammunition in the year 1795.

However, there's one small problem; Pickering didn't like democracy. In Pickering's eyes, and in the eyes of many New Englanders, democracy had allowed such injustices as the three-fifths compromise; the compromise which enabled Southern states to increase their representation in Congress by counting three-fifths of their slaves as population. Democracy was allowing unfair advantages to the South and there was only one way to resolve the problem; secession, Northern secession.

In 1804, Pickering led a movement to have the New England states break away from the United States of America and form a Northern Confederacy. The plan also called for Nova Scotia, New York and Pennsylvania to join the new country. Fortunately, the plan fizzled and Timothy Pickering lost his chance at the only position which seemed to elude him; there would never be a President Pickering.

The members of the Corps of Artillerists and Engineers at West Point in the late 1790's could be viewed as the first unofficial students of the military academy, which would not be officially founded until 1802. Not only was artillery training required for these men, but drills and tactics which were generally relegated to the infantry. Service along the frontier required a well-rounded soldier; an artillerist usually did not have the opportunity of conveniently transporting his cannons through the wilderness and taking the time to chose a suitable location to position them.

Captain Thompson recognized the value of this training and correctly anticipated the important role a military academy at West Point would play in the future of our country. A few months before he joined the garrison at West Point, he wrote to a friend expressing his thoughts and feelings on the matter.

Thompson on Governor's Island to Major John Stagg of the War Office:

My dear friend

Mr. Lovell presented your favor of introduction yesterday, he staid with me a few hours and was to depart from New York this day for Boston he obligingly gave me the arrangement of the Battalions and acquainted me of the Assemblage at West Point, this Sir, will be advantageous to us as a Corps, contemplated to be of Use to our country, their detachment from the too frequent allurements of publick Amusements and pleasures, will give that opportunity (if continued) to pursue that knowledge and experience that we have heretofore in this young and growing country perhaps unavoidable lamented. When the field is open for Science, when our government cherishes genius, may we not pleasingly anticipate the offering of American Engineers, assuredly we may -

It is clear that Thompson took pride in his country and his Corps and would continue to express his affection for both even after his release from the army in 1802. He also took great pride in his family and during his years at West Point his daughter Margaret was born. This peaceful time together with his family was to be relatively short-lived, however, for by the autumn of 1798, Thompson was once again on the move. This time he accompanied a detachment of the Corps to the frontier; Fort Niagara at the mouth of the Niagara River by Lake Ontario.

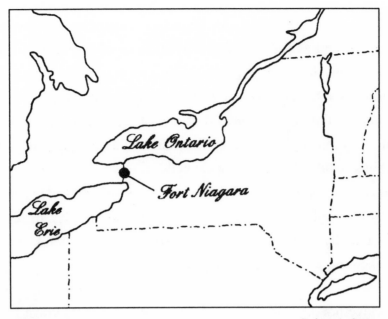

Robert A. Strong

Courtesy of Brian Dunnigan, Old Fort Niagara.

Reconstruction of The Gate of the Five Nations, which was the entrance to Fort Niagara in the 1790's.

When Thompson arrived at Fort Niagara in October of 1798, he was not entering the gates of a new American fort. The French were the first to put a military post there and constructed Fort Conti at the location in 1679. The structure was replaced by Fort Denonville in 1687, but it wasn't until 1726 that a fortification of enduring quality was built. The powerful Iroquois nation had consented to allow the French to build a stone

28

house at the location for the purpose of trading. However, the French seized the opportunity and stretched the trading house into a strong fortification. Known as the "Castle", the structure looked like a house in apparent compliance with the wishes of the Indians, but was cleverly designed to be "impervious to musketry" and had "dormers which provided positions from which defensive fire could sweep the ground around it."[15] This "House of Peace"[16] became a citadel of war and the designer, de Lery, did his job well; today the Castle is the oldest building in the eastern interior regions of North America.

Possession of Fort Niagara was to pass from French hands to the British in 1759 during the French and Indian War and the transition was not a peaceful one. The New World fort would succumb to an Old World siege which saw an unrelenting British bombardment for nineteen days and nights. During the ensuing years of British occupancy, the fortifications were repaired, enlarged and strengthened.

During the Revolutionary War, the fort was to become a launching point for combined British and Indian raids in New York and Pennsylvania, often pitting former neighbor against neighbor as fleeing Loyalists returned to attack the American farmers. These raids were to bring dire consequences to the Indians as American troops, in an attempt to bring an end to the Indians' armed support of the British, swept through their lands burning villages and crops. Facing starvation, many Indians sought food at Fort Niagara, and many died during the winter of 1779-80.

At the end of the war in 1783, the United States of America should have been able to immediately occupy Fort Niagara in accord with the Treaty of Paris. However, the British troops, Loyalist refugees and members of the pro-British Indian nations didn't see it that way. While many noble and patriotic reasons could be offered for the British reluctance to leave, there is no doubt that a strongly motivating factor was strictly economic; the highly lucrative fur trade. This trade in animal skins was viewed as a kind of four-legged gold mine and drew many fortune seekers (including Thompson in 1803) and Fort Niagara was a key center for that trade.

Remarkably, a combination of circumstances resulted in the fact that Fort Niagara was not occupied by the Americans until the summer of 1796. During the thirteen-year lag, the British, knowing that eventually they would have to relinquish the fort, did little in the way of building and repair[17]. They saved their efforts for the construction of Fort

---

[15] Dunnigan and Scott, Old Fort Niagara in Four Centuries, 1991.

[16] The term the French used to describe the structure when asking permission to build it.

[17] In 1784, the British commander of Fort Niagara received orders that *"No works whatever shall be undertaken on this side of the water."* (Dunnigan and Scott.)

George, which they built in British territory on the west side of the river immediately after evacuating Fort Niagara.

When the detachment of the Corps of Artillerists and Engineers arrived at Fort Niagara, they found eroding earthworks and cramped, run-down wooden buildings which presented more of a hazard than anything else. The new commander of the fort was Major J.J. Ulrich Rivardi, a skilled engineer who also had considerable artistic ability. Thompson had known Rivardi at West Point and would continue to correspond with him even after Thompson was transferred to Detroit.

Rivardi was appalled at the condition of the fort and the poor quality of British craftsmanship that went into it, commenting that it appeared as if they built *"their works in Such a Manner & of Such materials that they are Sure to be in constant employment as the repairs are constantly wanting"*[18] . However, when it was suggested that Fort Niagara be abandoned in 1799, Rivardi was influential in shifting the opinion to renovating and strengthening the fort instead, although he was not at Niagara long enough to see any improvements finally made.

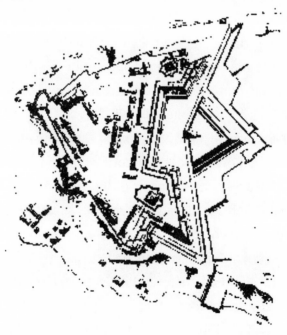

National Archives
Using his artistic talents, Major J.J.U. Rivardi drew
this map of the layout of Fort Niagara in 1798.

In May of 1799, after being at the fort for about six months, Captain Thompson asked Major Rivardi for leave so that he could return to his family in New York City and

---

[18] Dunnigan and Scott.

bring them to Niagara. However, because *"no other company officer"* was at Niagara, Thompson was *"not permitted by the Major to go for them"*; a situation which he confessed *"exercises me extremely"*. Thompson was informed that he could go only when Lieutenant Visscher from Oswego arrived to fill in. Visscher did not reach Niagara until August and it was not until September that Thompson began his journey. It must have been difficult for Thompson to wait as it is likely that the birth of his daughter Catherine[19] had occurred while he was away and he had yet to see his new baby girl. His greatest concern, however, was that yellow fever might take another family member in New York City, as it had taken his brother, William, the previous year.

Any parent dreading a long car ride with children should imagine what journeys were like in the 1790's. The trip from New York City to Fort Niagara would take a healthy man, traveling alone, weeks under the best conditions. Thompson was transporting his wife, a newborn and at least three other children with all their belongings across rivers and lakes and through wildernesses full of unknown dangers. However, the family must have made record time (or met Captain Thompson in Albany or Schenectady, which were mentioned as possible rendezvous points), because a payroll of November, 1799 indicates that Thompson was already back at Niagara. While there is no record of what transpired on this trip, there is a detailed and hair-raising account of the Thompson family's journey from Detroit to New York City in the winter of 1802.

Hopefully, the family didn't become too settled, because by May of 1800, they were on the move again, this time to an even more remote garrison in the Michigan[20] Territory, at Fort Lernoult[21] in Detroit. Detroit shared a similar history with Niagara; early French settlements taken over by the British and relinquished in turn to the United States. In 1701, Detroit's first fort was constructed by Antoine de la Mothe Cadillac, a rather colorful character who lacked a royal lineage and decided to take the initiative and created his own well-known coat of arms[22]. Cadillac had commanded at Mackinac, Michigan in 1694 and had become well acquainted with the riches to be made in the fur trade. This was probably the motivating factor for asking for a land grant, which he obtained in 1701 and promptly began the tiny settlement which would become the sprawling city of Detroit.

The fort, originally named Fort Ponchartrain, fell into British hands during the French and Indian Wars in 1760. In 1763, the British managed to withstand a fierce

---

[19] Catherine Thompson was born in 1799 and her tombstone indicates that she was born in New York City.

[20] From the Indian words "michi"- large and "gami"- lake.

[21] Captain Thompson spelled it "Lernault".

[22] Cadillac's name and coat of arms are used by the car manufacturer. It is ironic that a luxury car company adopted a bogus coat of arms as its symbol.

attack led by Chief Pontiac of the Ottawas, who was understandably angered by the continued loss of Indian lands. By 1766, peace treaties were signed with the Indian nations and the British settled in and started reaping the profits of the fur trade. Fort Lernoult was constructed in 1778 in an attempt to protect the region (i.e., the region's profits) from the rebellious Americans. Again, like in the case of Fort Niagara, the United States should have been able to occupy Fort Lernoult after the Treaty of Paris in 1783, but reluctant to relinquish the fort (i.e., the fort's profits), possession was not turned over to the United States Army until 1796.

If Captain Thompson could only use one word to describe Fort Lernoult, it would probably have been "isolated". Fortunately, unlike when Thompson first arrived at Fort Niagara, in Detroit he had his "*little family*" with him "*which makes this remote Situation from the Sea Coast pass more reconcilable then otherwise it might*". Travel overland was effectively nonexistent and travel by water was only possible during the months of good weather, which seemed precious few.

On April 26, 1802, in a letter Thompson addressed only to "*My Dear Friend*", he complains that "*We have been Shut out all the Season of inclemency from any Kind of information national or general, except what you had the goodness to express in your last* [letter]*, no mail from the postmaster Genl, nor are there any offices yet established here for the reception of letters, or newspapers -*". In April of 1801, Thompson wrote to Lieutenant Richard Whiley[23] at Michilimackinac (Michigan Territory) assuring him that whenever he received "*any news papers*" or anything "*interesting or entertaining, be assured you shall have them the first possible conveyance*". If news was scarce, pay was even more infrequent. "*The last payment here was up to 5th: Sept.*", Thompson wrote in that same April letter and informed Whiley that "*the paymaster was prevented reaching your garrison by the setting of the season*".

The remoteness and lack of accessibility to the forts in the Michigan Territory made it all the more critical that their defenses remain in good repair. This appears to be at least part of the reason that Captain Thompson was sent to Fort Lernoult, but apparently it wasn't soon enough. In September of 1800, Thompson wrote to Major Rivardi at Fort Niagara stating, "*I have compleated the casements of all the embrasures but thrice I wish the timber had been left entire until we came - as the measure and length of many were not correct, particularly the sills and some cap pieces, so that these repairs and the Magazine Guard are the duties Solely of Artillery -*"

---

[23] Whiley was also to become a friend of Thompson's son, Alexander Ramsay Thompson.

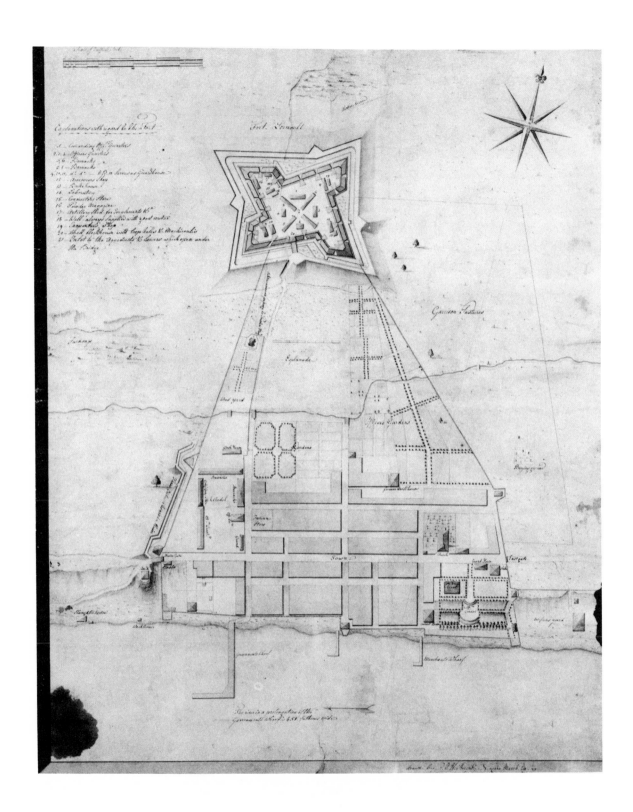

Fort Lernoult, Detroit, drawn by Major Rivardi in 1799. (Clements Library.)

Engraving of Michilimackinac from 1813. (Clements Library.)

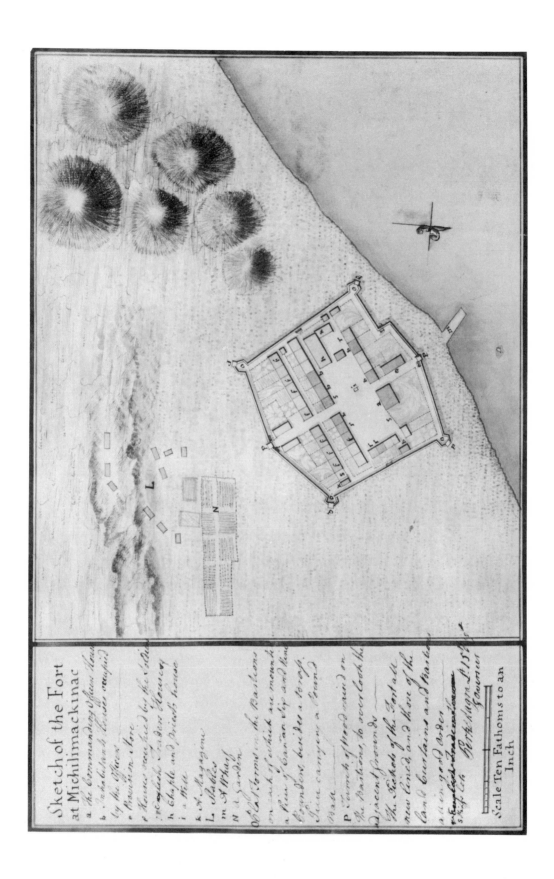

Sketch of the fort at Michilimackinac. (Clements Library.)

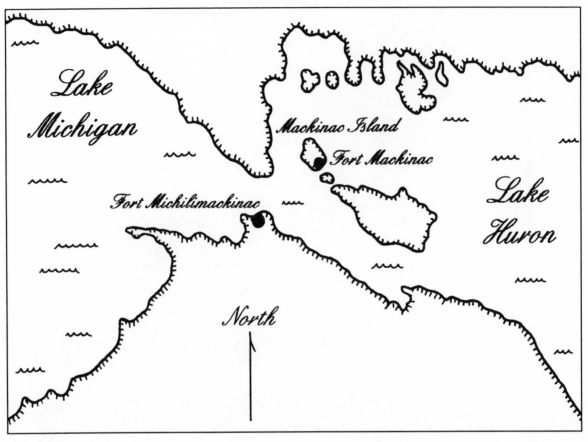

In the beginning of this letter, Thompson expresses his condolences over the death of one of Major Rivardi's children from smallpox. The following words clearly show that Captain Thompson, the professional soldier, was still first and foremost Thompson, the father.

...to lose so Sweet and promising a Child not only touches the Souls of their parents but causes the hearts of others to feel their afflictions. We have twice experienced those Sad and trying events, and which cannot be possibly expressed. We sincerely condole with you and your affectionate lady - calm reflections from the decrees of that power who gives and deprives us of our dear pledges, and which is not within human control, must Soothe their Sweet remembrance -...

Thompson appears to have been unusually sensitive to the feelings of others, even when it involved something as indisputable as the chain of command. In 1801, a reorganization *"annexed"* Lieutenant Whiley to Thompson's company and after informing the Lieutenant of the change, Thompson adds that *"how this event may affect*

Disease

The United States was not immune to the waves of diseases which claimed so many lives in European cities throughout the centuries, and although the types of diseases may have been different, their deadly impact was the same. A yellow fever epidemic in Philadelphia in August of 1793 decimated the population at the rate of 100 dead per day. Elected officials fled the city and the government came to a standstill until a temporary center could be set up in Trenton. Afflicted areas became virtual ghost towns. By the time the deadly tide subsided in November, 4000 lives had been claimed.

However, the terrifying disease would return again and again. In May of 1799, Thompson wrote from Fort Niagara to William Simmons at the War Department in Philadelphia and related that "*reports prevail here, that the Sickness so lately calamitous to your unfortunate City has again taken place. Permit me to express as at a former time, that it may not touch you or any you hold dear...*". These were not idle sentiments, for during one outbreak in 1798 in New York the fever "*proved fatal*" to Thompson's "*youngest brother*". The following year, Thompson wrote that he was "*permitted by Maj. Gen. Hamilton to go to New York or Albany for my Family*" and expresses his "*anxious desire to remove them*" from New York and bring them to Fort Niagara, lest the same fate befall his wife and children.

Yellow fever was characterized by jaundice and internal bleeding and was spread by mosquitoes carried from the Caribbean. Even though the epidemic began near the

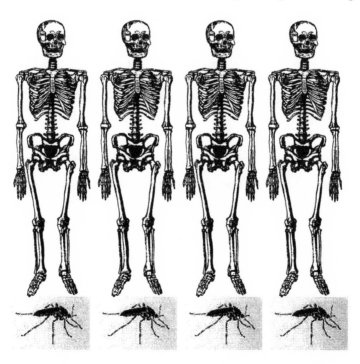

harbor, the connection was not made until the fever had struck not only Philadelphia several times, but Charleston, Baltimore, Boston and New York. Once the mosquito culprits were identified, ships from tropical ports were quarantined until deemed safe and the devastating epidemics finally ceased. In New York, the place of quarantine was Governor's Island, and yellow fever was not the only disease which was feared.

To Thompson on Governor's Island, June 23, 1795:

...if my recruits should reach you before my arrival...will you please restrain them from going into New York if they request permission - they may take the smallpox -

Smallpox had ravaged native American peoples after the arrival of the Europeans and was still claiming an alarming number of lives in the late 18th century. These terrible epidemics drove physicians like Edward Jenner to try to find cures. In 1796, Jenner gave the first vaccination to James Phipps. Today, thanks to doctors and scientists like Jenner, smallpox has been eliminated from the face of the Earth.

your feelings, I am not competent to Say, because we have never seen each other, thus much I will Say that nothing Shall be wanting on my part to make your Situation in my company every Way consistent and agreeable". It is unlikely that many officers inquire as to how the command structure "*may affect*" the "*feelings*" of their subordinates.

This reshuffling of companies was only the beginning of major changes to come and it apparently was causing no small confusion and uncertainty. Thompson refers to the lack of orders and information to his post as being due "*to the derangements of the executive departments and of the military establishments*" and by early 1802, he anxiously awaited news of the "*peace establishment*" which promised to greatly reduce the armed forces and would ultimately end his twenty-three years of service. Before that reduction occurred, however, Thompson was reshuffled into Moses Porter's[24] battalion.

Porter, who had just been promoted to Major, was congratulated by Thompson in a letter dated February 17, 1801. The letter discusses the new arrangement and suggests that America's reliance on foreign commanders was finally drawing to a close.

Country Men of my own, is what I have long advocated ought, And only ought to be in Service, the United States, has paid pretty well & dear for foreign Experiments, what have they amounted to, the event has Shown it, Ignorance, incapacity And peculation. No one under the heavens wishes the reputation of the American Artillerists more than I do, And I say it is within native reach...

---

[24] Porter was the first to raise the flag of the United States in the Michigan Territory in 1796.

The "*peculation*"[25] to which Thompson refers, may very well have to do with several earlier incidents involving Colonel Rochefontaine at West Point in 1798. During New York winters, firewood was a precious commodity and one which was strictly regulated in the army. In a letter dated February 2, 1798, Thompson describes in detail how "*Mr. Cronk*" was seen carrying "*to Colonel Rochefontaine two cords of wood*", when the allowance was only one and a half cords. This may seem like a trivial occurrence, but Thompson was a stickler for honesty and fairness and he no doubt knew that this was only one of many of Rochefontaine's abuses.

On March 24th of 1798, Thompson wrote to Lieutenant Horatio Dayton in Elizabethtown, announcing in a rare instance of sarcasm, "*that Colonel Rochefontaine in the plenitude of his power...transferred my company*" to Fort Niagara; a move Thompson was not happy about making. In the next paragraph, Thompson explains with some sense of satisfaction that "*A Court of enquiry was held here, on Colonel Rochefontaine, the beginning of this month, for hiring Publick horses & Waggon to the United States, and receiving the Proceeds - proof established and transmitted to the War Office, to be laid before the President, important must the issue of this as well as other causes be and extremely interesting to the American artillery, of which I will apprize you by the first post...*".

It is probably not by coincidence that Colonel Rochefontaine retired from the army only six weeks later, on May 7, 1798. It is unfortunate that a man who so ably aided our cause during the Revolution and was instrumental in beginning an academy at West Point, should end his career is such an ignoble fashion.

Many careers were to end when the long-awaited, and long-dreaded, peace establishment downsizing occurred on June 2, 1802. The reason behind this thirty-percent[26] reduction can be explained in two words; Thomas Jefferson. Victorious in the election of 1800, President Jefferson sought to curb what he saw as the excesses of power of the central government, of which, ironically, he was now its chief executive.

Jefferson was opposed to the continuation of a standing army in times of peace, preferring to have local militias confront any immediate crises until a regular army could be formed. His ideal would have been to have mandatory military training for citizens to create these militias, ready to jump to the country's defense in an efficient and disciplined manner. However, realizing that relying on the citizenry to maintain such high standards

---

[25] To steal or embezzle public property.
[26] The total number of officers and enlisted men in the army fell from 4051 to 2873.

of preparedness was an impractical goal, Jefferson resigned himself to maintaining an army, albeit a smaller army.

On the positive side for the armed forces, Jefferson decided that if there was to be a United States Army, it was going to be the best possible, so on March 16, 1802, an act of Congress finally officially created the United States Military Academy at West Point. Jefferson believed that the American soldier should be useful to his country in times of peace as well as war, and with the skills learned at the Academy, soldiers could be called upon to build roads and forts and explore and survey new territories.

For Captain Alexander Thompson, Jefferson's reforms meant he would have to explore new job possibilities. When news of the reductions finally reached Detroit, Thompson wrote to his "*dear Friend*" at Niagara (possibly Major Porter?) on June 20, 1802, and even though his own livelihood was gone, Thompson still shows his characteristic concern for the well-being of others.

...the Military peace establishment of the United States was communicated here, by express, Via Pitts-burgh. As to myself I am perfectly reconciled because I have a comfortable home to go to, but I lament the fate of many, not so Situated in life.

What works here, discharges in plenty and the pay spending, - not a little bit of an uproar, ...hurry and bustle is the day here, - I have been so effected with the Rheumatism in my back, that I have been unable to help myself for some weeks, - Am enabled to walk a little, have taken comfortable rooms in town, and Shall Stay in the neighbourhood of my Garden[27] at Mr. Pettins house, untill the Middle or latter end of August, when I shall pay you a Short Visit, with the rest of my friends at Niagara, and proceed with my dear little family to New York...

Partially crippled by rheumatism and without income to support a wife and six children, Thompson made preparations to enter the civilian ranks for the first time in his adult life. On August 6, 1802, Thompson sent letters to both his brother Johnny and Caleb Swan, Pay Master General, attempting to get his affairs in order.

From Thompson to Swan in Washington:

---

[27] There are several references to gardens in the documents. Fresh fruits and vegetables were precious commodities, especially for Army families, and it appears that travels were often postponed until after harvests.

Having become a Supernumerary Officer on the peace establishment of the Army of the United States I take the liberty to forward to you a Power of Attorney to receive the pay allowed for my service...I have to request you will be pleased to pay my Brother Mr. John Thompson No. 310 Broadway City of New York...As I love my country I wish my Successor more ability and better health...

To John Thompson in New York:

...I wrote you under date of 16th: July, And then Stated my Situation and intentions - finding the Seasons advancing, and the hazard that may attend the passage of three lakes -Erie, Ontario, & Oneida and the North River communication, I think it advisable to leave this country in all this month. I mentioned to you in my last that the final Settlement of my claims was to be by Power of Attorney to the Seat of Government, in consequence of Which, I have enclosed to you power properly executed to Caleb Swan Esq - Pay Master General...I shall receive Captains Pay for my Services in the Artillery last War - Which will give an additional Sum of five hundred Dollars and More - I have committed this power and letters to be delivered to you by Mr. Chas. Currie Merchant of this place, my friend, and most extensive in the fur trade, I believe he is in concern with Mr. Astor, any civility you and the family Show him will oblige me...we shall sell all our Stock & furniture as the expense of transportation So many hundreds of miles will cost a great deal, and our own expenses must be considerable. I shall announce to you our arrival at Niagara by post with the day of our departure from thence. Amelia is busy fixing the children...Amelia and the Children Joins me in love to you each of the family and the dear boys[28]...

Delays resulted in the Thompson family not leaving Detroit until the end of September; a month's difference which almost cost their lives.

To Caleb Swan, January 22, 1803:

I did not leave Detroit with my dear little family untill the latter part of September. The polite attentions of Colonel Hamtramck[29] and the officers of the garrison

---

[28] John Thompson never married and had no children of his own. Captain Alexander Thompson's eldest sons, John and William, probably lived in New York with their uncle and attended school or worked.
[29] Thompson's commanding officer at Detroit and future acquaintance of Major Alexander Ramsay Thompson. A portion of Detroit is named after him.

to me and my family will ever merit my warm acknowledgments. And the reception and kind treatment of Major Porter and the officers of his garrison will claim my greatful remembrance. Our trip to Oswago in an open boat was difficult and Hazardous owing to Violent Storms that had closed the creeks commonly calculated for harboring and obliged us to beach the boat thru Several times in one attempt, at the Second Swell of waves about eleven miles from the great Sodus the boat filled, Mrs. Thompson and my children were taken out without any other accident then compleatly wet, the loss of Some of our Stores, and the injury of our clothes and baggage - the Snow at the time 2nd: Nov. five inches on the level, we Soon had large fires to dry ourselves - fifteen nights my dear little family laid in a tent on the Shores of Lake Ontario, we remained Sometime at Oswago and Utica (old Fort Schuyler) for chances of boats to get along, it was not until the beginning of last month that I arrived in this my Native City [New York] *from this tedious and expensive Journey. I took Violent cold but am now happily recovered...*

Having survived his harrowing journey, Thompson immediately began to seek ways of adding to the moneys already owed him by the government. In a letter directed to Henry Dearborn[30], Secretary of War, Thompson relates the story of his hazardous trip from Detroit and then comments with mixed emotions, that *"Notwithstanding, Sir, I was Superceded by an officer of inferior rank, I love my country, and Sincerely wish the reputation of the American Artillery - I shall ever be partial to a profession I assumed in defence of my country in my youth".*

Thompson continued by mentioning matters of pay and asks for compensation for duties, such as Pay Master, he performed at Fort Niagara. *"I have to request you will be pleased to direct the allowance of Sixteen dollars per Month to pay masters to be remitted to me,"* Thompson explains, *"for the discharge of those duties. I am led to this request from the very great expense attending the removal of my family from Detroit to this City without an alternative to me -"*

Perhaps it had been Thompson's desire to take up some sort of business in New York City and remain in his *"comfortable home"* there, but it was not to be. Whether there weren't any opportunities for an ex-artillery officer in New York or the sedentary life was simply not for Thompson was not recorded, but in any case he was on the move again after only a few months. He would return to the frontier posts at Niagara and

---

[30] Dearborn had served with distinction during the Revolution, but was an ineffective Secretary of War, noted for embracing Jefferson's cost-reduction plans which depleted the army's resources. A city in Michigan is named after him.

Henry Dearborn was Secretary of War from 1801 to 1809. He corresponded with Captain Alexander Thompson about official business, especially when Thompson was Military Storekeeper at West Point.

"I am very respectfully Sir, Your Ob[edient] Ser[van]t H Dearborn"

Detroit where he had gained valuable knowledge in one other area besides the military; the fur trade.

In the August 6, 1802 letter to his brother John, Thompson explains that Mr. Currie, a merchant in the fur trade, would deliver the letter in person and stated that "*any civility you and the family Show him will oblige me*". With the benefit of hindsight, it appears that by bringing the merchant and his relatives together, Thompson was trying to arouse interest in the trade with his brother, and any other potential investors. This letter, as well as several other pieces of correspondence, also refers to Mr. Astor; John Jacob Astor, the man who would effectively monopolize the fur trade and become the richest man in the country.

Astor was one of America's greatest success stories. At the age of twenty, he left his native Germany for New York City, arriving in 1783. For four years he held various odd jobs, including a stint as a baker's boy. Around 1787, he turned his talents to the fur trade; a career move rarely equaled in the annals of American business. However, not content with the fortune he made in furs, Astor invested heavily in farmland. Normally, such investments only brought modest returns, but this farmland happened to be in the heart of Manhattan. It is estimated that Astor's business dealings netted him over $20 million[31]; a hefty sum to which his capable descendants would substantially add, establishing one of America's family dynasties.

Based upon his connections with Astor's company, his acquaintance with traders and Indians and his knowledge of the frontier, Thompson apparently succeeded in convincing his brother that there were sizable profits to be made in the fur trade. While men like Astor were making millions, Thompson's aspirations were no doubt more modest; providing for his wife and children would have been sufficient. In addition to his brother John, there was a second investor in the venture, Franklin Robinson and Company (where John was employed as a bookkeeper), and between the two they provided Thompson with the thousands of dollars necessary for the trip which would last over a year and a half.

Thompson's detailed and meticulous records of expenditures begin in Albany, New York on July 1, 1803; if there was one thing he had learned in the army, it was how to keep track of every penny. The accounts provide a wonderful record of the grueling process, and considerable expense, of traveling before the era of the train. Boatmen had to be paid to cross every river, canal or creek. Carters were needed to carry supplies at every step. There was the expense of sleeping and eating at roadside inns, when they were

---

[31] To make a comparison, in 1803 the Louisiana Purchase, which effectively doubled the size of the United States, cost only $15 million.

The beginning of the detailed record of "*Account of Cash Paid by Alexander Thompson*" for his journey to Michilimackinac.

available. In addition to exhausting stagecoach rides over bumpy roads through mud and choking dust, there were unforeseen adventures such as being "*detained by rock caveing in*" or "*boat sunk below the falls*".

A letter from Thompson to his investors at the beginning of the trip illustrates a typical day of the journey.

Gentlemen   *Fort Stanwix (Rome)*
                                                July 13, 1803

I had the honor to acquaint you in my letter of the 3rd: Instant of my intention to have ascended the Mohawk River on the fourth, that day being the Anniversary of American independence. No more could be done then loading the boats, from the arrival of boats that descended the River I found the Waters low, instead of One large boat Capt. Walton furnished two Smaller Sending things on to Niagara that made their Weight equal without any alteration in the conditional price that I mention'd at Sunrise on the Morning of the fifth we left Schennectady and Arrived in the canal here last evening about Sun set. from the Want of Rain the Mohawk is remarkably low, but by persevering labour we passed Several rifts, the canal at the little falls is now in repair And we were necessitated to have the goods and boats carried...the constructing lock one half mile from this canal obstructs the passage of the Water until this afternoon when we shall be let out and proceed for the Oneida lake. Should the lake be favorable I hope to be at Oswago the next day...

45

Despite these numerous obstacles, Thompson arrived in Detroit in early August. This fact is evidenced by some of the government red tape which had to be cut through before Thompson could get down to business.

Paid Treasurer Indiana Territory for Licences to Vend
Merchandize 15th: Sept. 1803 - for one year...

Paid Treasurer Indiana Territory for Licence to Vend
Merchandize 15th: Sept. 1804 - for one year...

Paid Collector of the Customs Detroit for Permit to land invoice...

After the August expenses, the record skips to December. An entry for December 2, indicates that Thompson took lodgings in Detroit at the home of John Dodemead. A December 20 entry records that Thompson paid "*Dr. Wilkinson Ballance of his Account for Medicine, attendance, and advice from 17 Augt. to 21 Sept.*"; not surprising, considering Thompson's health was poor even before embarking on his long journey.

Although his final destination was intended to be Michilimackinac, on the Straits of Mackinac between Lakes Michigan and Huron, and right in the heart of the fur trade, it is also not surprising that the onset of winter forced Thompson to remain in Detroit as months of bad weather kept any vessels from sailing. He did report to his investors that during the winter, he "*had done as much business as any one here, and to as great Advantage*"[32] , but there are no records as to what that business might have been. On May 2, 1804, the accounts pick up again with carters, furriers, pelt sorters and ship captains. During that month, Thompson finally continued on to Michilimackinac and in a letter to resident Dr. Francis La Baron, Thompson discusses the details of the business.

"*The invoice of goods herewith is placed into your hands to be Sold on the best and Most Advantageous terms for Peltries of every kind, of good Quality and in Season, Deer Skins excepted, as also for cash or good bills on Montreal that may be taken in payment for Peltries, you will be pleased to give a preference to beaver, otter, Bear, Martin, & Racoons, and it may be Necessary for you to be governed by the prices I would not wish to exceed Beavers 15/- Otters 4 Doll., largest Size - Bears 8 Doll. Martins 9/*

---

[32] From a letter belonging to the Thompson family.

*Racoons 3/6- Mratts 2/ minks 3/4- fishers 6/ fox & Catts 3/6- both grey and red fox, and as much under those prices as you may be enabled to effect, Buffaloes I wish to omit untill I am advised in New York - When you have a Sufficient Number of Skins to make a pack be pleased to have them put up in good order Marked **AT**, and numbered at Same time make an invoice expressing the quality and quantity of each pack your long residence here will enable you to avail of many advantages that will be equally so to each of us, tho the prices in the invoice left with you are moderate you will take Such advantage of the Sales as may be best, the invoice as Assorted Amounts to fifteen hundred and Seventy two pounds Eleven Shillings, New York Currency equal to three thousand Nine hundred and thirty one Dollars, thirty Seven and a half Cents, and for your agency I will allow a Commission of five per Cent, the expence of Storage and making of pack you will place to my Account as some Small adventures may and will arrive before the general return of the Tradeing Gentlemen I wish you to Keep your eye on them and do the best, Should you be so fortunate as to be able to get Some packs on the return of the first Vessel from Detroit, be pleased to Ship to Capt Ernest Collector of that port for my Account with a letter of advice, that I may be enabled to Keep forward as early as possible...*

Thompson was understandably anxious to return to his family after an absence of over a year and equally anxious to avoid "*some Small adventures*" and return before bad weather set in and caused a repeat of his last journey back to New York. His confidence in Dr. La Baron's business acumen was obviously not misplaced; three days after the letter, Thompson and his pelts were finally on their way home. Leaving Michilimackinac on October 18, he arrived back in New York on December 10; happily with no record of sinking ships or cave-ins.

At this point, the document collection falls silent; not a single letter, accounting statement or scribbled note exists for the year 1805. Knowing that Thompson was a diligent record-keeper for every business transaction or crisis, it can be surmised with some degree of assuredness that nothing of any major importance occurred that year. Although he probably was not aware of it at the time, there were precious few years remaining in his life, so hopefully this lack of documents meant that Thompson was finally able to live quietly and peacefully with his family, at least for a little while, with the profits he realized from his fur expedition.

The documents which left off with furs, pick up again with nails and paint brushes in the summer of 1806. On July 27 of that year, Alexander Thompson returned to West Point to become Military Storekeeper; a position which would clearly have been too tempting for him to refuse. From the age of seventeen, his life had been the army and Thompson's zeal for his new position is evident in the meticulous records he once again began to keep.

That Thompson was the right man for the job is not only apparent from his own work, but it is also obvious from the words of his friend Captain Richard Whiley. Whiley had been transferred from Michilimackinac to Thompson's old command on Governor's Island at the new Fort Jay[33]. While the particular subject of Whiley's letter (below) isn't stated, Thompson's handling of the situation and the nature of his character are conspicuously illustrated.

My Dear Friend,   *Fort Jay 20th October 1806*
...I am too well acquainted with your correctness and indefatigable disposition to suppose that the public property would continue long exposed, to the injury of the wheather, after it had been intrusted to your care / You are too much of a military man for that...

Unfortunately, this devotion to duty and unwavering honesty would pit Thompson against Major William A. Barron at West Point in December of 1806. The conflict appeared to revolve around confusion about the payment of a bill; specifically, Barron denied being paid the sum of $52 even though Thompson had produced Barron's signed receipt for the money. According to affidavits of witnesses involved, it may very well have been the case that Barron simply forgot being paid and that Thompson misconstrued the situation. However, in a letter to William Simmons at the War Department, Thompson alludes to some darker motives on the part of Major Barron.

" I enclose for your perusal the following correspondence between Major Wm. A. Barron and myself. And add to this, I did refuse to him [Barron], as well as the cadets, public Keys, and public property.. "

The letter further explains that in addition to attempting to gain personal use of public property, Major Barron also requested some kind of under-the-table deal in regards to repairs on his house and promised Thompson that for the favor *"he would furnish me with Wood and Vegetables - (little did he Know the late little Captain[34]) my reply was I would do what was right, but not by purchase -"*. Based upon these incidents, Thompson

---

[33] Fort Jay was completed in 1801.
[34] On two occasions, Thompson referred to himself in this manner.

continues, *"he has declaired he will ruin me and my family"*; a threat which may have manifested in Thompson's dismissal in 1808.

According to Major Barron's letters, he is completely innocent of any wrongdoing and claims that the incident regarding the payment of the bill was simply all a misunderstanding on Thompson's part. And *"With respect to the Threat you conceive my letter conveyed, you mistake. I meant not to convey a Threat. - Threatening would be inconsistent with that fairness and gentlemanly Conduct I intend to preserve in my Correspondence. The impeachment of my reputation I ought to consider a <u>precious</u> thing. My life is dear to me; but, my Character is dearer --"*.

After restating in detail the chronology and conversations of the incident, Barron concludes the letter of December 29, 1806 by stating that, *"I expect, Sir, that you will acknowledge your mistake, and express your regret for all that you have said injurious to my Character relating to this affair. - This acknowledgment and expression of regret, will be honorable on your part; to accept it will be honorable on my part; & satisfactory to me. Nothing short of it will be satisfactory."*

Thompson, with his *"correctness and indefatigable disposition"*, stood by his claims and in a letter to Barron, declared, *"Never while I breathe will I cease to be Candid."* Thompson then restates his version of the affair and concludes that, *"I have only to Say, you are mistaken. Never will I say another word, untill imposed on me."*

Unfortunately, the affair did not remain private between the two men and in fact was brought before the Secretary of War, Henry Dearborn. There is no mention in the documents of any decision from Dearborn, but Thompson did request that his friend Simmons at the War Department, intercede on his behalf and ask that Dearborn *"suspend his opinion"* as *"Colonel Jonathan Williams of the Engineers, who is a great professional Character"* will *"give his opinion respecting my conduct in the repairs and duties of my office"*.

Colonel Williams had been appointed by Thomas Jefferson to be the first superintendent at the Military Academy at West Point. Williams had been chosen for his scientific rather than military knowledge and although he was a great advocate of discipline, he was also an advocate of compassion. There is no evidence of whether or not Williams was able to influence matters in Thompson's favor, but he was to play a key role in the destiny of the Thompson family in July of 1808.

In the mean time, there was an academy to build, and to constantly repair; an academy considerably different from the modern image of a noble institution in which everything is ruled by discipline and order. The document collection contains complaints from master carpenters and laborers for overdue bills. Even as classes were beginning, windows were still being glazed and walls were being plastered. There was a request from Thompson to Dearborn for approval of a contract *"drawn & Witnessed by Major Wm. A. Barron"* to build a wall, *"to prevent the herds of horses & Cattle from grazing on the plain - and doing injury, as we have not Sufficient Guard to prevent it"*. Apparently, the War Department did not have a standard procedure for dealing with cows and Thompson asks Secretary Dearborn *"to be pleased Sir to instruct me how to act in this case -"*.

Many of the contractors involved in the construction of the Military Academy were from Newburgh, New York; a city twelve miles to the north of West Point on the Hudson River. During the Revolution, Washington had his headquarters in Newburgh[35] and it was there that he announced the end of the war. Newburgh was to become a center for manufacturing and its proximity to the Academy brought business to its contractors and merchants; merchants like John Brown who immigrated from Ireland and set up a "Universal Store" which claimed it could supply everything from hardware to jewelry, including glass, Bibles, gin and groceries.

---

du Pont

Alexander Thompson to Secretary of War Henry Dearborn, August 24, 1807:

...Shipped on board the Schooner Jane of New York, Mr. Briggs Belknap Master, Eight hundred barrels of Powder, as invoiced, to be remanufactured, Addressed to E.I. du Pont de Nemours & Co. Wilmington State of Delaware...

As part of his duties as Military Storekeeper at West Point, Thompson conducted "proofs of powder"; tests to determine the strengths of different lots of gunpowder. Such determinations were crucial as every lot of powder was different and an artillerist couldn't accurately calculate where his shot would travel without knowing the strength of the powder. Apparently, an entire shipment of 800 barrels of gunpowder failed to meet specifications and Thompson was forced to return it. An average company might have staggered from the cost of remanufacturing and re-shipping an order of this size, but this was not an average company.

Pierre Samuel du Pont de Nemours fled the horrors of the French Revolution and came to America. His son, Eleuthere Irenee, founded the company that began producing gunpowder in 1802. The company eventually branched out into high-explosives and chemicals and Du Pont & Company became the largest chemical company in the world.

However, the family did not limit themselves to simply supplying the military. Pierre du Pont's grandson, Samuel, fought for the Union during the Civil War as a Rear Admiral in the Navy. E.I. du Pont's grandson, Henry, finished first in his class at the U.S. Military Academy at West Point, where, hopefully, the powder never again failed the test.

---

[35] From April 1, 1782 thru August 18, 1783.

Among the numerous receipts in the document collection is a bill from June of 1807 for *"One hundred and twelve Dollars - for Bell for the Military Academy with all fixtures"*. Every good school, especially a military school, needed a bell; unfortunately, *"not having the funds to meet this Bill",* the bell-maker had to wait for his money until the War Department could clear a check. Money was scarce in the early years, and respect from the government even scarcer. As a result, Superintendent Williams twice resigned; his frustration deepened by the lack of books, equipment, housing, teachers and even cadets[36].

Although the fledging Academy threatened to die in its infancy, Thompson was greatly encouraged by the sight of young cadets preparing for the future. He expresses his feelings to Superintendent Williams in a letter dated June 9, 1807.

...Sir, I feel a pride, tho in a Subordinate degree, that the youth of my country are So anxious to Know that profession, that my early years led me to Study and practice of for the independence of our dear country. Permit me to assure you, that my heart grows warm, when I see with my Own Eye, the dear Native youth promising to be American Engineers and Artillerists -

---

An Insult

At the end of a letter to William Simmons at the War Department, dated August 5, 1807, Alexander Thompson remarks to his friend, *"I am happy to hear, and to read, that Natives of our dear Country - Will not admit of insult, come from where it may -".*
The *"insult"* to which Thompson was referring is an incident known as the Chesapeake-Leopard Affair.
On June 22, 1807, the British ship, H.M.S. Leopard, came alongside the United States frigate, *Chesapeake*. Commodore James Barron of the *Chesapeake* was informed that as part of the Royal Navy's search for deserters, his ship would be boarded. Mired in indecision (for which he would later be court-martialed), Barron did not call the crew to readiness and when the Leopard's cannons blazed to life the ensuing battle was little more than target practice for British gunners. While the Americans fired only a single shot before surrendering, their ship was riddled with no less than twenty-two holes blasted through the hull. There were twenty-one casualties among the American sailors and four crewman suspected of being deserters were taken aboard the Leopard.

---

[36] The first class in April of 1802 contained only 10 cadets. Originally, there were no requirements for admission and students ranged from a 12-year-old boy to a married man with children.

War seemed inevitable, but President Jefferson held back and instead fired off an economic salvo. In early July, Jefferson ordered all ports closed to British ships. The move was aimed at hitting the British in the most painful spot; their wallets. Unfortunately, the British continued to harass American shipping and the war Jefferson hoped to avoid was only delayed until 1812. However, those five years gave young Alexander Ramsay Thompson time to graduate from West Point and personally answer the "*insult*" about which his father had written.

Thompson's enthusiasm led him to volunteer his services in training the cadets "*when duties of my office permit, Cheerfully will I tender my little ability to their improvement in the Cannon, Howitz & Mortar practice*". Such artillery practice must have been a refreshing diversion from the reams of paperwork with which he had to contend. As always, however, Thompson faithfully attended to all his duties and as a result once again faced legal problems; a writ was served against him by disgruntled contractors who wanted the government to pay its overdue accounts.

From Thompson to Simmons at the War Department, Washington, August 5, 1807:

...on your advice I informed Misses Powells your result, that their Charge of Use respecting the exchange, will not be admitted, they Say compulsory means Shall compel them to relinquish - Geo Gardiner & Son on my advice to them, interest would not be allowed on their accounts, immediately had a Writ Served, I have given bail - this is very Unpleasant, and affords Small returns for my exertions to put the Public buildings in tenetable repair - I shall Write the Secretary of War on this to Morrow Via New York -

As if facing another lawsuit for performing duties for the United States wasn't bad enough, in September of 1807, Thompson received a letter from his old friend Perkins in Washington, hinting at worse things to come. Perkins had gone to that city to try to obtain a good position, but quickly realized "*that instead of being in any way of Obtaining an appointment, I think my Coming here most likely to prevent it, that is should it be thought Convenient for the accommodation of others to Continue me in my present subordinate Station, I have little reason to expect that merit or long Service will have any weight*".

It is evident that politics was a ruthless art from the earliest days of government and Perkins continues by warning Thompson that he might become another victim of those same politics.

... but enough of Complaints, I have another Subject which though of the most delicate nature I beg you to excuse me for introducing. I should not be your friend and should not deserve your Confidence should I neglect it. the Subject I once took the liberty, though unpleasantly to mention, and I beg leave to entreat you to be Circumspect, being on the Spot and interrogated as I have been you will allow me to form some Oppinion - pray Sir listen to the Voice of a friend, I am afraid your Case is determined upon, there has no doubt been some who have done you no good here. The Subject is too delicate I dare not Continue it, but pray Sir for the Sake of your Amiable family to be on your Guard and as this may perhaps be the last act of friendship that may ever be in my power to perform for your advantage I am Sir solicitous that you should profit by it. I Beg of you Sir to do so you are perhaps not Sensible of your Situation...should I hereafter learn anything of important concern I will not fail to give you notice - the Secretary of War is here himself, so that my intimations have Come from a Superior Source -

What was the nature of this subject which was so delicate that Perkins dared "*not Continue it*"? Were Major Barron's threats finally coming to fruition? Unfortunately, any attempts at an explanation would only be speculation. The facts remain that the government was painfully slow in resolving a debt which put Thompson under personal hardship and by June of 1808, he would lose his position as Military Storekeeper.

Though continuing with his normal duties throughout the period of the suit, the stress finally seems to have gotten the better of Thompson, as is evident in a letter to his lawyer, Charles Baker of Newburgh, dated November 19, 1807.

"In the Name of goodness what can the matter be, that your Letter of the 26th of Oct. was not delivered me Untill Saturday 14 Nov. to Whom did you deliver it, or in Whose charge was it placed. business of this Nature Should be prompt. As my Attorney you advise payment of Geo Gardiner & Sons Debt for the United States, with costs of Suit, my good Sir, What is Amount of their costs. Some Specific Sum must be named, or government will not pay..."

The government apparently did not pay until February of 1808, putting Thompson through seven months of hell. In a note to Simmons dated February 23, 1808, Thompson expresses his gratitude to his friend for helping to avoid the dire consequences had the account not been settled.

"Acknowledgements of all I hold most dear in Saving me at this moment from the horrors of a prison..."

The affair left the family financially and emotionally depleted. Yet even as they struggled to regain their footing, an even more severe blow struck.

To (Callender Irvine?), Superintendent of Military Stores, Philadelphia, June 14, 1808:

he [Secretary of War Dearborn] *says Capt. Jon. Snowden has been approved of as my Successor, And that my Services in that capacity will cease, on the first of June, this event was both Sudden and unexpected, the appearance of the Stores and Magazine will demonstrate wether I have discharged the duty with industry and professional ability. To become Supernumerary when one of the oldest Captains of the American Artillery on the peace establishment at Detroit, having Served my country in the revolutionary War, Well Known personally and professionally by your Worthy father, Now to be deprived of my office, having an amiable Wife and Six Children, I can with great truth Say, I have been unjustly dealt with...I have only to say that no motives have ever been mine, but the love, the good, and the best meant intentions for my country -*

For all Thompson's *"best meant intentions"* and long service to his country, he was now destitute, desperate and understandably bitter toward a government which seemed to value none of his qualities. However, he apparently harbored no ill will toward his successor and actually invited him into his home, but not without some very practical motives. In addition to probably receiving some amount for room and board, Thompson reports to Captain McLean in New York that he had *"Capt. Snowden for the present to board with me by which means I hope to Save my garden for the Summer."* With so many mouths to feed and no income, every vegetable was precious.

In July, the merchant John Brown of Newburgh, wrote to Thompson demanding payment for his personal account. Thompson's reply was that due to *"the cruel and unjust treatment I have met with from my government...I have not money to Send for butter or Snuff"*. The state of the family was indeed pitiable and Superintendent Williams could not stand by and watch their condition worsen. In a letter[37] to Secretary of War Dearborn dated July 26, 1808, Williams details the plight of the Thompsons.

---

[37] Biographical Register of the U.S. Military Academy, George Cullum, 1891.

You would certainly be moved to compassion were you to see him in his reduced state, surrounded by a respectable though indigent family, - his wife, a woman of an amiable mind, but in delicate health; a blooming daughter (Amelia), about eighteen; a son (Alexander), about fifteen; and two daughters (Margaret and Catherine), twelve and nine, without an assistant of any kind in the family...Could you have this painful scene before you as I have, I repeat you would be moved with compassion, and I feel assured that I may rely upon a favorable answer to a request I am about to make; it is to give Captain Thompson's son, Alexander Ramsay Thompson, a cadet warrant, to date August 1, 1808, as the intermediate pay is of importance to this poor family.

Cadets were given an allowance for food of approximately fifteen cents a day; a paltry sum, especially for an entire family. However, it seems that even this tiny amount was to be denied them, because Academy records indicate that Alexander Ramsay Thompson did not become a cadet until November 21, 1810. There are no records to indicate how the family managed through the winter of 1808-1809, but by spring of 1809, Alexander Thompson is again writing receipts and keeping accounts for the Military Academy, this time in the position of Assistant Military Storekeeper, no doubt a position acquired with Williams' help. Those few documents written in the spring and summer of 1809 would unfortunately be the last pieces of correspondence from Thompson.

On September 28, 1809, at the age of fifty, Captain Alexander Thompson died at West Point. The cause and manner of his death is not known, but it would not be unreasonable to surmise that poverty, legal entanglements and a lifetime of military service with all its hardships were contributing factors. He was buried at the cemetery in West Point and left behind his "*dear little family*" without any means of support.

Fortunately, the Superintendent once again interceded, giving Thompson's widow permission to board twelve cadets. It is sadly ironic that after devoting his life to his country, Captain Thompson's family is best remembered at West Point for his wife's cooking. The privilege of dining at the Widow Thompson's became highly sought-after; cadets "willed" their privileges to other cadets upon graduation.

The reasons why this privilege was so jealously guarded is evident; food at the mess hall was prone to mice, roaches and decay, not to mention that the cadets were under the perpetual scrutiny of officers. Dining with the Thompsons not only meant good food, it gave the cadets a chance to unwind in a relaxed, family atmosphere. The three Thompson daughters, Amelia, Margaret and Catherine, never married and when their mother died (probably in the late 1830's) they retained the right to board cadets.

Thompson House, West Point, New York.

This was a situation unique in the history of the Military Academy and it continued until 1878 when the last surviving daughter, Amelia, died at the ripe old age of eighty-eight. The Thompson's house, which was the last surviving structure from the Revolutionary War era, was demolished shortly after Amelia's death. Today, the site of the Thompson house is somewhere under the Military Academy's swimming pool. Mrs. Thompson and her three daughters are buried next to Captain Thompson in the eastern end of the cemetery. Next to their graves is a tall monument bearing the name of the son who would bravely carry on the family tradition, Lt. Col. Alexander Ramsay Thompson, and the small stone of his wife Mary, who turned out to be as much of a fighter as any of the Thompson men.

Chapter 2

"Remember The Regiment"

Lt. Col. Alexander Ramsay Thompson, 1793-1837. (Courtesy of Thompson family.)

"Received West Point Oct. 18th: 1806, from Alexander Thompson two dollars in full, for Work done, in making a coate and pantaloons for his little Son Alexander - William Rodney"

This is the first known reference to Captain Thompson's youngest son, Alexander Ramsay Thompson. Born February 19, 1793, Alexander Ramsay's early years were no doubt filled with stories of his family's struggles and triumphs during the Revolutionary War. In addition to army stories, those years were also filled with army posts from the bustling city of New York to the remote frontier of the Michigan Territory.

At the age of three, Alexander Ramsay lived on the military post at West Point. At six years old he was at Fort Niagara, at seven Fort Lernoult, Detroit and at thirteen he was once again at West Point where he stayed until graduating from the Academy at the age of eighteen. With such a childhood, it isn't surprising that Alexander Ramsay Thompson chose the military for his profession. Years later, his widow Mary would write that from the time he became a cadet, he had *"a firm determination to devote his Life to the service and interests of his Country"*. However, even if Thompson had other aspirations, the family's financial difficulties would have been a strongly motivating factor toward becoming a cadet, and subsequently a career officer.

Upon graduating from the Academy on January 3, 1812, young Thompson was promoted to First Lieutenant of the 6th Infantry. Like his father before him, Lt. Thompson was to see action in a war while still in his teens. In June of 1812, after years of rising tensions between the United States and Great Britain, President James Madison and Congress finally declared war. However, this would not be a war like the Revolutionary War or the Civil War. This war was unusual. Even the name, the War of 1812, points to the fact that there was not a single, clear-cut reason for the war.

This sketch by A. R. Thompson is the only known representation of the Post Hospital at Fort Mackinaw, constructed in 1827 under Thompson's direction. The hospital burned down 10 days after its completion.

In fact, there were many reasons, some of which actually did relate to objectionable conduct by the British; the continued harassment of American shipping, impressment of seamen and a general contempt and disrespect for the United States and its citizens. Events such as the Chesapeake-Leopard affair in 1807 had left strong anti-British sentiments throughout her former colonies and incidents continued to occur which only exacerbated the situation.

Of course, a war is seldom fought which has no underlying economic reasons and the War of 1812 was at least similar to other wars in this regard. Once again, America was caught in between the mighty forces of the European power struggles; specifically the ongoing war between France and Great Britain. Both countries tried to restrict the United States from trading with their enemies which resulted in substantial economic losses for Americans. For years, prohibitive shipping laws enacted by the British had the most severe consequences and the United States government decided to fight fire with fire with its own restrictions. The result? Americans got burned even worse; burned to the point of bankruptcy in many cases.

Considering that the majority of the businessmen and sailors who suffered from British policies were from New England, it would not be unreasonable to conclude that this region was enthusiastically supportive of the war. However, just the opposite was the case. Many New Englanders were vehemently opposed to a war; in part because a war would effectively eliminate what little trade remained. Also, by 1812, Napoleon had earned a reputation as a tyrant and people in the northern states sympathized with the British and their allies.

Great Britain didn't need another war on its hands either; Napoleon and the Grand Armee were sufficient opponents. Sensible of this fact, and perhaps equally sensible of the fact that hurting American shipping also hurt themselves, the British government announced that it would repeal the restrictive laws. This news was announced by the British Foreign Minister on June 16, 1812. Unfortunately, news traveled slowly and unaware of the British policy change, Congress declared war on June 18.

America's Paris

When comparing any city to Paris, one would probably consider its architecture, art and romantic atmosphere. When looking at these factors, it isn't likely that a match would be made between Paris and Baltimore in 1812. However, Baltimore earned the nickname *"America's Paris"* not for its beauty and sophistication, but because of the mob violence that occurred there which was akin to the bloody savagery of Revolutionary France.

Barbaric riots took place after a newspaper, the *Federal Republican*, published anti-war sentiments. Initially the publisher, Alexander Hanson, was simply threatened. When threats were ineffective, his office was destroyed. However, Hanson continued to publish the paper and in July an angry mob besieged his new office, threatening to kill Hanson and everyone with him. During the fighting which ensued, one of the mob's members was killed. News of the death spread quickly, the mob's numbers swelled and it appeared as if a blood bath was imminent. The local militia and city officials were reluctant to aid Hanson, but finally persuaded him and his comrades to go to the jail under the promise of protective custody.

Not backing up that promise with troops, the mob quickly broke into the jail and dragged out Hanson and about a dozen of his friends and supporters. Among those dozen men was Henry "Light-Horse Harry" Lee, a daring cavalry commander during the Revolutionary War. (At the time of the riots, Lee was the father of a five-year-old boy who would also make a name for himself in the pages of military history. That boy was Robert E. Lee.) For several hours, Hanson, Lee and the other victims were viciously beaten, stabbed, tarred and feathered and had hot wax poured into their eyes. All of this occurred while some officials locked themselves in their homes and refused to help. Miraculously, Hanson survived, but never fully recovered from his injuries and died several years later at the age of the thirty-three. Lee also never recovered from his injuries and died in 1818.

The Baltimore riots during the War of 1812 were dark days in American history, but, unfortunately, they would pale in comparison to the New York riots during the Civil War.

Ostensibly, had the news reached the American shores earlier, the war would never have begun. Realistically, the people along the frontiers and in the south probably would have found some other reason to start a war. What was it that would have driven these people to fight? Land; land to the south, land to the west and land to the north.

To the south was Florida, owned by Spain, an ally of Great Britain. To the west were Indian nations, supported in their right to the land by the British. To the north was Canada, a nice chunk of land which many Americans thought would make a great addition to their country, but was currently owned by the British. If there appears to be a pattern developing, it was a pattern which certainly was not overlooked by the expansion-hungry citizens of the United States of America.

As the War of 1812 began, many people had high aspirations about its results. A young lieutenant in the 6th Infantry, fresh out of the Academy, probably also had high aspirations for himself and his country. However, Thompson's earliest campaigns could not have been tremendously encouraging. Records[38] indicate that Thompson was "on the Northern Frontier, 1812, - in General Wilkinson's Descent of the St. Lawrence River, 1813, -and in the Campaign of 1813-1814, on the Lake Champlain line of operations, being engaged in the Battle of Plattsburgh, N.Y., Sep. 11, 1814".

The campaign along the "Northern Frontier, 1812", was intended to be a sweeping, three-pronged attack upon Canada. What began with hopes of conquering Canada ended with America losing Detroit, Fort Dearborn, Michilimackinac and in addition, lost an army's worth of soldiers who had been taken prisoner. To rub salt in the wounds of defeat, the outcome might have been different if the army had been supported by the militia units who had refused to cross the border in defense of their own country's fighting force.

"General Wilkinson's Descent of the St. Lawrence River" in 1813 was another failed attempt to invade Canada, specifically Montreal. The year 1813 also saw the loss of Fort Niagara and the burning of Buffalo. Fortunately, American spirits were bolstered by naval victories on the Great Lakes, thanks to men like Commodore Oliver Hazard Perry, renowned for the report, "We have met the enemy and they are ours". On land, however, leadership was lacking and like the Civil War, it would take about two years to weed out the bad generals and find the competent ones.

One bad general was clearly James Wilkinson and it is a mystery how he stayed in a position of authority for so long. During his illustrious career, Wilkinson had secretly tried to have George Washington removed from power, conspired with Aaron Burr to seize the southwest and form a new country and then turned on Burr and testified against him, was on the Spanish payroll as an agent for its government and was prone to alternating fits of depression and euphoria, most likely aggravated by heavy opium consumption.

Fortunately for the country, by 1814, Wilkinson was out and leaders like Winfield Scott, Andrew Jackson and William Henry Harrison (the latter two going on to become Presidents) came to the forefront. Despite the country's poor leadership in the early years, Lt. Thompson also proved his merit, which was later to be described by his widow, Mary. During the war, she claimed, Thompson, *"tho' but a youth, in many instances Honorably distinguished himself:- in command of 100 men he gallantly defended a bridge, which the enemy was endeavouring to pass."* While it would be easy to dismiss a widow's words as exaggerations, one could hardly doubt the words of Major General Alexander Macomb, Commander-in-Chief of the United States Army. In 1844, General Macomb wrote about the bravery Thompson exhibited throughout his life, especially at a bridge which led from the town of Plattsburgh to Fort Munroe during the Battle of Plattsburgh in the War of 1812.

---

[38] Cullum.

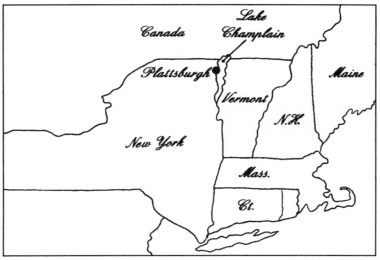

Robert A. Strong

Even before the battle, his bravery and abilities must not have gone unnoticed, because on May 1, 1814, Thompson was promoted to the rank of Captain at the age of twenty-one. Ten days after his promotion, Captain Thompson was involved in the Battle of Plattsburgh, where he was to prove himself once again. The battle was an American victory, due to a clever maneuver by Master-Commandant Thomas Macdonough on his ship, *Saratoga*, on Lake Champlain. Macdonough positioned his anchors so that during a crucial moment in the battle he was able to quickly spin the *Saratoga* around, bringing a fresh battery of cannons to face the British, who ultimately surrendered their fleet.

The American fleet defeating the British during the Battle of Plattsburgh.

63

Seven months later, the War of 1812 was to end, on paper at least, on December 24, 1814, when the Treaty of Ghent was signed. The treaty named no victors, bestowed no conquered lands and after over two years of fighting, only called for the restoration of the way things were before the war. However, as the war never should have begun, so should it have ended earlier. News of the treaty had not reached the British or American forces in Louisiana by January 8, 1815, the day the Battle of New Orleans occurred. General Andrew Jackson won the day for the Americans, in addition to winning fame for himself, and even though America's high hopes for conquest had been dashed, the battle ended the war on a relatively high note for its supporters.

General Andrew Jackson's (1767-1845) popularity helped him win two terms as President of the United States.

The treaty had called for all occupied territory to return to its pre-war ownership. Part of that occupied territory was Fort Niagara and on May 22, 1815, American troops once again garrisoned its battered walls. Among those troops who returned that year was Alexander Ramsay Thompson. However, the fort he knew as a child and the fort he returned to as a Captain in 1815 must have appeared quite different. Structures were gone or decaying and the water was encroaching dangerously close to the walls. Elaborate plans were drawn up to repair the fort and the seawall, but as the threat from the British diminished, so did the government's interest in Fort Niagara.

Like his father before him, Alexander Ramsay Thompson was now a Captain at Fort Niagara. Unfortunately for posterity, however, while he shared his father's devotion to the military, he did not emulate his record-keeping skills. The elder Thompson carefully wrote duplicates for all his correspondence, leaving over a hundred documents

Courtesy of Brian Dunnigan, Old Fort Niagara.

Cannon at Fort Niagara, cast in 1815.

Courtesy of Brian Dunnigan, Old Fort Niagara.

South redoubt of Fort Niagara, as it appeared in the 1790's.

behind. In comparison, only a few letters remain written by the younger Thompson and the following may provide some explanation as to the reason. [39]

Captain Kearny at St. Louis to Thompson at Sackets Harbor, May 22, 1820:

...I penned a few lines, which I did hope...might form the groundwork of a steady correspondence - I was mistaken - [40]

Kearny at Greenbush, N.Y. to Thompson at Sackets Harbor, April 22, 1821:

Whether you owe me a letter, or I owe you (tho' by the bye, I believe the former is the case)...

Lt. Hunztelman at Fort Brady to Thompson at Jefferson Barracks, August 11, 1834:

In garrison when officers could communicate personally with the commanding officer, you always preferred verbal to written communications...

The documents in the Ricca Collection concerning Alexander Ramsay Thompson were predominantly written to Thompson by his friends and by his widow to relatives and government officials. Yet even from these, it is possible to gain insight into his remarkable character and trace the equally remarkable sequence of endless forts and army posts which stretched the length of his all-too-brief life.

While army life often involves frequent moves, Thompson and his long-suffering wife, Mary, seem to have had more than their share, as his service record indicates:

1815-1818	Fort Niagara
1818-1819	Recruiting Service
1819-1821	Sackets Harbor
1821	Greenbush, New York
1821-1823	Fort Brady, Michigan
1824-1825	Recruiting Service
1825-1826	Fort Niagara
1826	Fort Howard
1826-1828	Fort Mackinac
1828-1832	Fort Gratiot
1832-1833	Fort Mackinac
1833-1834	Fort Leavenworth, Kansas
1834	Jefferson Barracks, Louisiana
1835-1836	Recruiting Service
1836	Fort Jessup, Louisiana
1837	Florida, Seminole War

---

[39] It is possible there were more letters which were lost in the fire of 1858, or by some other means. It is also possible that there are others yet to be discovered.
[40] Thompson family document.

The People Back Home

While a soldier's life is difficult, it can be equally difficult for his family waiting and worrying about their loved one. The following letter to Captain Thompson painfully illustrates one family's anguish.

Philadelphia July 23.1817

Honable Capt. Alex. R. Thompson

Dear Sir

With Humble Respect, I beg leave to address a line, in requesting the favor of Your Honor to be kind enough to inform me concerning a Brother of mine by the name of Charles Cress, in the 2d. Reg. US. Infantry, under Your Honors Command. in his last Letter dated in June 1816. he informs me of his intention of coming home at the expiration of his term of 5 Years service which would end in May last. but as we never have heard from him since, makes his poor Mother & family very much distressed in Mind, fearing his Death or some accident has befel him.

Could we merit Your Honors attention to befriend us with any information relative thereto, it would be esteemed with heartfelt Gratitude by his disconsolate Mother and Relations, and merit a lasting obligation of thankful remembrance for the same.

I am with submission,
Honable Sir.
Your Respectful
Humble Servant
Alexander Cress

The documents begin in February of 1816 with a letter from Captain Shell at Sackets Harbor and addresses Thompson's concern about being transferred from Niagara. It appears that the concern stemmed from a personal transfer Thompson was contemplating; that of bachelor to married man. Shell assures Thompson that he "*need not be apprehensive of being removed from Niagara. - And now my dear Sir, Since every obstacle is removed, you may indulge yourself with the pleasing thought of a matrimonial connection.*"

That connection occurred on April 29, when at the age of 23, Alexander Ramsay Thompson married the 26 year-old, Mary Waldron Nexsen at the Dutch Reformed Church in New York City in a ceremony conducted by Philip Milledoler, who was to be a lifelong friend of the Thompsons. Mary was descended from Dutch book printers who came to New Amsterdam (New York) in the early 1650's when Peter Stuyvesant was governor. The family became prosperous farmers in Brooklyn and Manhattan and held many important official positions. William Robert Thompson, Alexander's brother, also married a Nexsen, Janette Nexsen, although it isn't clear whether Janette and Mary were sisters, cousins or some other relation. It also isn't clear when the Captain and Mary had their only child, but it is recorded that the boy died in infancy.

In November of 1816, Captain Kearny at Sackets Harbor sent his regards to Thompson and the new Mrs. Thompson. However, niceties aside, the bulk of the letter concerns an element crucial to military operations; the washerwoman. Washing clothes for an army was an exhausting, low-paying job and one in which many low-ranking soldier's wives were employed to help make ends meet. Washerwomen were always in demand, but apparently not always promptly paid for their services. Captain Kearny informed Captain Thompson at Fort Niagara that a Mrs. Niblock was seeking payment for washing she did for Thompson's men while the 6th Infantry was at Sackets Harbor[41] in 1815. Regrettably, there is no record as to the outcome of Mrs. Niblock's dilemma.

Captain Kearny also wrote, "*In about a fortnight we move to our new Barracks - They are not completed - we are to pass our winter in them (which by the bye, has already commenced, having now tolerable sleighing) we shall then move into Tents, viz in the Spring & finish the building in handsome style. The architecture is good & handsome & is no little ornament, to this increasing in civilization town.*"

The barracks to which Kearny referred were to be christened Madison Barracks, presumably after the President of the United States, and were built in an elegant, Federal style; an enviable place to inhabit considering the rundown condition of places like Fort Niagara. In January of 1817, Major W. J. Worth at Sackets Harbor wrote to Thompson describing the barracks and the less-than-subdued celebration which followed their completion.

...we had quite a fete on moving in the barracks, received their name under a salute from the Fort & fire as well from the Regiment - after which a numerous party partook of a celebration - It being on the 8th Jacksons victory was likewise celebrated...It will be impossible for me to give you an idea of the Barracks, they are indeed splendid, extensive and commodious & superior to any in the States - or perhaps any where else - no person would conceive it possible to rear such an extensive fabric in so short a period & with so much elegance - & the most gratifying Consecration is, that they were built by soldiers -

During the year 1818, Captain Thompson was put in the recruiting service and was able to return to the city of New York where he and his wife had many relatives. Recruiting service seemed to have been a highly prized position; especially by Mrs. Thompson years later, when after two decades of endless movement, she pleaded with the likes of General Winfield Scott to bring her husband home from the frontier and give him a recruiting position.

---

[41] While stationed at Sackets Harbor in 1815, Thompson survived a post-war, army reduction, similar to the one which eliminated his father's position in 1802. The only change which seems to have occurred for Thompson was that he was transferred from the 6th Infantry to the 2nd.

Currently, Madison Barracks is an *Historic Resort Community*,
on Worth Avenue (named for Major Worth).

Courtesy of Robert Brennan

Sackets Harbor, New York.

In 1819, after about a year of the desirable recruiting service, Thompson headed back north, back to Sackets Harbor where he would finally be able to enjoy the famous barracks about which he had read so much. While there, he received a letter from his friend Captain Kearny who had been transferred to the *"Western Wilds"* of St. Louis in the Missouri Territory.

The Indians on the latter river have been lately growing rather troublesome; have murdered 2 men of Mautons Compy, *5th. Infy at Rock Island & I understand have threatened to attack the recruits...These are the "Winnibago's"[42], the most fierce & warlike any of the Tribes in the Western Country - They must however be put down & I presume Govt will take decisive steps for the same. It was reported a few days since they had attacked some Forts, on the river - this report however is incorrect.*[43]

Captain Kearny would eventually require *"3 months to recover, from indisposition"* after a year of service along the frontier. Such service was physically, as well as mentally, draining and Kearny added that the recuperation time back in New York also gave him the opportunity *"to reaquire a little civilization"*. During his years of military service, Thompson would also suffer with bouts of "frontier fatigue", occasioned by long marches, bad food, inadequate shelter from the elements and rampant disease. However, due to his single-minded determination, i.e., his stubbornness, Thompson continued in his duties despite poor health, as his widow recounted years after his death.

Mary Thompson to Dr. (Momer?), January 20, 1842:

You will no doubt recollect the feeble State of Col Thompsons health on his arrival to New York in the early part of the Summer of 1823 - This was occasioned by the injury he received in his Knee-joint while in actual duty, in Superintending the erection of public works at Sault St Marie when he was compelled to apply for a leave of absence in order to come to New York where he might avail himself of the Sea air & Sea bathing - Before leaving the Sault, he was in the habit of using crutches and Sometimes, when Suffering from blisters he was carried upon a litter *by two men in order to visit his working parties - He continued to use crutches for about 18 months. Dr. Wright Post of NY, who was in the habit of visiting him, told him it was "an injury which would probably affect him during life", which proved true & he was generally afterward obliged to use a cane, and frequently on Marches & fatigue he Suffered much from it - in fact, the injured limb never recovered its former size, nor strength - and in Florida it troubled him much, as he often had to move through swamp & mire in a charge.*

In fact, the last charge which cost Thompson his life, probably shouldn't have occurred. His widow Mary explains:

---

[42] The once-friendly tribe eventually lost their lands, several times, finally settling in Nebraska. Other American Indian tribes would continue to be a 'problem' for the United States until the end of the century; the problem being they were in the way of land-grasping white settlers.
[43] Thompson family document.

Suffering much privation, loss of Health and enduring great hardship and fatigue - yet notwithstanding he never relinquished his command, nor suffered himself to be placed on the sick report. When the Campaign under Colonel (now Genl) Taylor commenced its march from Tampa, he was urged to remain, being considered too much enfeebled in health to undertake the march - but he absolutely refused, stating that he could not consent to remain absent from his Regiment, and that he would not give up as long as he could keep his seat in saddle.

While it is again tempting to dismiss such accounts as exaggerations, both official records[44] and numerous pieces of correspondence attest to the fact that Alexander Ramsay Thompson was an officer of exceptional abilities and qualities; qualities untainted by personal ambitions or "*Politicks*" for which he did "*not care a pinch of snuff*". Letters from fellow officers speak of his "*reputation for vigilance*", his dedication to duty and a compassionate character which prompted a Lt. Gallagher to relinquish his comfortable post in Maine to serve under Thompson on the frontier at Mackinac, even though Gallagher admitted to knowing "*next to nothing about the place.*"

While places like the Michigan Territory were still considered to be in the wilderness compared to the east coast, the nature and boundaries of the frontier changed dramatically during Thompson's life. By 1820, settlers were streaming into the new states of Indiana, Illinois, Mississippi and Alabama. While the country was blessed with numerous waterways, they didn't stretch everywhere and farmers and merchants began demanding easier and less expensive ways of transporting produce back east and finished goods to the ever-expanding west.

Part of the answer was a road; not merely a clearing through the wilderness with a couple of ruts worn by wagon wheels, but a stone-covered highway complete with bridges and drainage systems. Such a road was begun in 1811 in Cumberland, Maryland and continued for over five hundred miles to Vandalia, Illinois. When the first section of the Cumberland Road was completed in 1817, it provided something never before possible outside of the developed areas of New England; a safe, cheap way of traveling overland.

The year 1817 also saw the beginning of an even greater feat of engineering, the Erie Canal. Two wars with the British and years of experience had taught the inhabitants of New York State that if they were to remain competitive with their goods, they also needed more secure and effective travel routes; specifically a water passage from the Hudson River to the Great Lakes. However, to many early 19th century minds, merely the idea of such a monumental project was considered to be nothing short of the fantasy of a madman. However, thanks to the firm determination of visionaries like Governor De Witt Clinton, the plan succeeded despite the tremendous odds.

When the 362-mile canal from Buffalo to Albany was completed in 1825, the once exorbitant costs of transporting goods from the Lakes to New York City plummeted as much as thirty times. While businesses thrived and towns sprang up along the new waterway's route, the Erie Canal actually had a negative impact on Fort Niagara, where

---

[44] Including an account of Thompson's gallant actions in Florida written by General Zachary Taylor, who was to become the 12th President of the United States in 1849.

The Officers Stone Quarters at Fort Mackinac. Construction
of the building was begun in 1780 and completed in 1799.

The West Blockhouse of Fort Mackinac, constructed in 1798.

A Window of Opportunity

When Brevet Major Alexander Ramsay Thompson was stationed at Fort Niagara from 1825-1826, he may have been a witness to a bizarre, yet fascinating and valuable, series of experiments. The experiments involved a Canadian trapper by the name of Alexis St. Martin, who had been the victim of an accident in John Jacob Astor's American Fur Company store near the fort in Mackinac three years earlier. There, he received a gunshot wound to the upper abdomen from a shotgun at close range. The fort's physician, Dr. William Beaumont, was called to the scene and after tending to St. Martin, assumed that the wound was fatal.

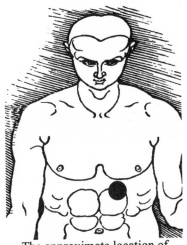

The approximate location of
Alexis St. Martin's wound.

However, St. Martin beat the odds and survived, but his survival was a mixed blessing as the wound, which literally formed a hole into his stomach, refused to heal. Only a small piece of skin covered the opening which could be drawn back like a curtain. Dr. Beaumont quickly recognized that by drawing back that curtain of skin, he had before him a marvelous window of opportunity; a window into the mysteries of human digestion. Beaumont convinced St. Martin to accompany him to Fort Niagara in 1825 where the doctor published his first report on the series experiments which would last for several years. Conducting no less than 238 experiments, Beaumont performed tests to measure the speed of digestion by placing pieces of meat or vegetables on strings and lowering them into the stomach through the wound and pulling them out at various intervals.

In 1833, the results of all of these experiments were published in a landmark work of human physiology, *Experiments and Observations on the Gastric Juice and the Physiology of Digestion*. While Dr. Beaumont received international recognition for his work, St. Martin was probably content to simply live through it all and not die until he was an old man.

Brevet Major[45] Thompson was stationed when the canal was opened.

Since goods now flowed freely along the canal, completely within the borders of the United States, the strategic importance of Fort Niagara as a defense for American interests declined. In fact, it declined so sharply that the government decided to remove the garrison from Fort Niagara and close its gates. It must have been with mixed emotions that Bvt. Major Thompson marched away from the fort he had known for almost thirty years. Although Fort Niagara was put back into use two years later and would continue to be an active post into this century, there is no record of Thompson ever returning.

Yet despite the continued construction and improvement of roads, bridges and canals, travel was still not without dangers and hardships. With the advent of the highway came the highwayman. Though often greatly exaggerated, stories of Indian attacks still struck terror in the hearts of settlers and long-distance travelers. However, in the list of possible hazards, Mother Nature still topped them all.

To Major Thompson from General George Brooke, Fort Howard (Green Bay, Wisconsin), May 13, 1832:

We reached this post yesterday, only having made, a most stormy passage, I began to think at last that the water Gods of Lake Huron, intended to forbid my passage across their dominions; but honest industry, & good seamanship, we, at last prevailed...

To Major Thompson at Fort Mackinac, from Lt. Jamieson at Fort Brady (Sault Ste. Marie, Michigan), March 2, 1833:

It is with pleasure I can inform you of my Safe arrival at home after one of the most fatiguing marches I have ever had in my life...I presume Lt. Gallagher has presented you with a detail of our little dangers as well as of the some that Miserable, cold and gloomy night we had of it, on the island of Saint Martine [near Montreal]. While thus surrounded by difficulties, amidst storm and cold snowy winds of a tempestuous night, I must confess I had ample leisure to reflect upon my situation and to ask if this was pleasure. There was still enough to be thankful for as our lives had been spared in crossing the Lake...It has often been said that there is no picture of imagination which has not been surpassed in wonder by the realities of life, and I fully believe it. And as a proof of it, I would almost declare that our journey across was even beyond conception...

To Major Thompson in New York City from Major Brant in St. Louis, January 7,1834:

You wish me a pleasant winter here, but I assure you this is almost impossible...the cold is now ten below zero...

---

[45] Thompson received the promotion on May 1, 1824 for "Faithful Service Ten Years In One Grade". The brevet rank was essentially an honorary one; while it included some increase of stature, it provided no additional pay.

In a letter from William Robert Thompson to his sister-in-law, Mary, dated April 28, 1836, it isn't clear if storms were to blame for Mary's troubles, but it is certainly a possibility considering that the Great Lakes region was infamous for its sudden, treacherous weather.

We received your long communication some days since giving an account of your painful & distressful Journey from Gratiot to Detroit, we felt it must have been one of the most trying times in your life...

As bad weather often hampered or delayed traveling, outbreaks of disease still initiated it. In the same letter from William Robert Thompson, he informs Mary that "*Mother Nexsen & Elizabeth have gone to Tappan* [New York] *to stay until the health of the City will warrant them to return*". With the terrible results of the smallpox and yellow fever epidemics of the 1790's still fresh in the family's memory, it isn't surprising that some of the Thompsons chose to flee to the countryside when the "*health of the City*" was questionable.

Beyond the cities, as the country's borders continued to expand, so did the scope of the diseases which were encountered. Poor sanitation was not uncommon along the frontier, especially at army posts, and in 1833, a consequence of these unhealthy conditions is evident in a letter to Major Thompson in New York. Thompson was to be transferred to Fort Leavenworth, Kansas, but on April 15 his friend, Major Brant, warned that Thompson should delay his journey as "*the 'cholera' & Fever is now taking off from 8 to 10 of a day*".

"Your friend & Serv[ant], J.B. Brant"

Thompson appears to have heeded this advice as he passed his year at Fort Leavenworth with no mention of serious illness. However, some of Thompson's colleagues did not fair as well, especially as regiments of soldiers began pitching their tents along the mosquito-infested landscapes of the south. The "*Fever*" was to become a serious threat to maintaining manpower strength, as was the steamy climate which the soldiers from the northern states had never before experienced. Lieutenant Sevier in Louisiana, wrote to Thompson in August of 1837 complaining of both of these problems.

...I was attacked with chills and fever and confined to my bed...I am getting out of humour with the Southern climate...

Although Thompson seems to have been spared any major illnesses, he was to eventually fall victim to the cumulative effects of the bad weather, long marches and numerous "*privations*" of the southern campaigns. However, despite diminished health from the hardships of duty, the deeply religious Thompson felt blessed to be able see the expansive beauty along the length and breadth of the frontier. Placing his fate in God's hands, he appears to have believed that any personal discomfort was a small price to pay for the unique opportunity of viewing nature in its most pristine state. Perhaps Thompson felt this way because he recognized that unspoiled wildernesses were rapidly dwindling and that beauty was being trampled underfoot by ugliness; an ugliness which took many different forms.

The following letter written by Major Thompson to his fourteen-year-old nephew, the future Reverend Alexander Ramsay Thompson, gives a wonderful insight into the Major's character, as well as insight into the struggles and values of America in the 1830's.

Camp Sabine La.
April 28, 1836.

Dear Alexander

Having a few moments of leisure I have devoted it to answering your letters, and to tell you that I feel a deep interest in your welfare.

You will perceive , we are now beyond the range of Post roads & post officers : as we are encamped on a fine ridge near the Sabine river, from which our camp takes its name - We have made a beautiful place of our canvas city, which contains fourteen companies of Infantry, and a field battery of Artillery, over which I have the Honor of the immediate command - our station is healthy and is well provided with a fine spring of water - We have left most of the trees stand as they grow by the wishes of the Almighty - and have cleared up all the underbrush so that we have a fine circulation of air, and a most delightful shade - At night our camp reminds me of the tales of the fairies, or the work of enchantment - ...

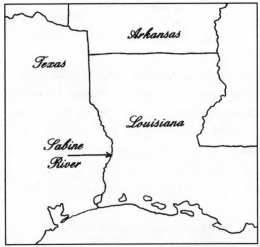

Robert A. Strong

The people of Texas are in a dreadful state; They are moving constantly before the Spanish Army, and flying for their lives, our road is lined in places with their cabins and temporary shelters and the country is consequently infested with robbers and pirates -

When I ride out any distance from camp, on my good horse, which is called Sabine, from the river in which he sometimes drinks: I always belt on my loaded pistols, and saber as I would in an enemy country : and would no more hesitate to shoot down a man, than to kill a snake if his conduct was threatening - The people of Texas grieve at leaving that country, and often remind me of the Jews weeping over Jerusalem; - They say that with those feelings of emotion, "We will not give up Texas" - "We will return and die in Texas" - "Texas is a beautiful country" -

We are not yet alerted as to the operations that may be required of us; and are waiting for circumstances to inform themselves - We hope these things may yet be peaceable...

I have a very fine and gentle horse, whom your aunt has named Sabine, and whom I constantly accustom to stand the music and fire of our guard, so as to learn him to stand the fire of the enemy if we should ever have one -

We have been a thousand times told of the murders of the Spaniards, but most of the stories now afloat, are made by the large land speculators, who get their living by falsehood - This country abounds in poisons, and our men have been bitten by the rattle snake, the scorpion, and the centipede, but all have been cured - The wood tick is very troublesome, as it gets under the Skin and creates inflammation ; and the red fly is worse-

I hope you seek every opportunity of improving your mind and manners, and let me impress on you that a modest and unassuming deportment, even more for a young man, than any thing else; it is beautiful in the female character, but equally so in a young man :- I hope you may cultivate this quality...let the Bible be your book of regulations, and then when you lay down to die, you will have a support, that man can not deprive you of.

It is due to your parents and family, that your name should not be sullied; and your reputation should be kept as pure as the mountain snow - let your order of nobility be, the nobility of the mind, cultivated in the paths of Virtue & Integrity-...

Affectionately Yours -
Alex. R. Thompson[46]

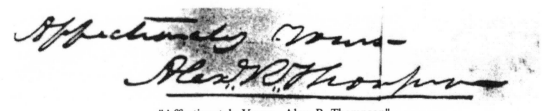

"Affectionately Yours - Alex. R. Thompson"

Thompson's thoughtful and insightful words to his nephew bear a striking resemblance to the sentiments of Thompson's father, to whom virtue and integrity were the cornerstones of his personal ideals. These words may also have been prophetic, as

---

[46] Thompson family document.

The Piano

One of the drawbacks of moving frequently is that many personal belongings and pieces of furniture will eventually be damaged or lost. Mrs. Thompson complained that their move from Louisiana *"to Florida, destroyed all our effects by mildew, damps, and other means"*.

In 1821, when the Thompsons were moved from Greenbush, New York to Fort Brady in Michigan, they transported what must have been a particularly precious item, their piano. The man responsible for its transportation wrote:

"Thy Piano was for the day I recd. it, forwarded to Schenectady very carefully in a waggon without other loading - with special instructions to the transporter situation to the tender feelings of that instrument..."

The piano apparently continued to travel with the wandering Thompsons as they moved around the northern frontier for a dozen years. However, when orders arrived to go to Fort Leavenworth in Kansas, the decision was made to leave it behind.

Detroit Aug. 28th 1833

Dear Major

I have the pleasure to acknowledge the receipt of your letter, and hasten to answer your two enquiries. In regard to the Piano, it was thought unadvisable to sell at auction, as there are no purchasers here of that article. except, when they procure a new one. Mr. Brooks, by my advice, called in a person most competent to appraise it, and he valued it between 50 & 60 dollars, and a Gentleman from his Majesty's dominions, happened in and proffered fifty dollars, and we thought best at once to close with him.

There is no record as to the reaction of the family piano falling into the hands of the British.

Thompson family.

Colonel Thompson's sword (hilt above, close-up of engraving on blade below).
The sword was a standard issue for general and staff officers from 1832 until 1850.

Thompson family.

79

A Dreadful State

When Thompson wrote that *"The people of Texas are in a dreadful state"*, he was referring to the plight of the Texans who were fighting for their independence from the government of Mexico. Though the fighting was fierce and bloody, the road to independence was relatively short, considering that American settlers had lived in Texas for less than a generation.

During the 1700's, Spaniards had set up missions across Texas, but few settlers took advantage of the vast region. Then in 1820, the Spanish government granted Moses Austin's request to begin colonies. Austin died before being able to carry out his plan, but his son, Stephen, directed the establishment of the colonies which consisted of several hundred people. In 1822, Mexico gained its independence from Spain and the new Mexican government allowed the colonies to grow, expecting it would be a slow process.

However, by 1835, the number of new Texans had swelled to over 25,000; a large percentage of whom exhibited the American penchant for independence. A year earlier, Antonio Lopez de Santa Anna had overthrown Mexico's constitutional government and he acted as any new dictator with an upstart colony would; swiftly and brutally.

From February 23 to March 6, 1836, Santa Anna led the siege of San Antonio at a small, former Franciscan mission known as the Alamo. Behind the walls of the Alamo,

187 Texans (including Davy Crockett and Jim Bowie) faced 4000 Mexican troops. When the walls were finally breached, only half a dozen Texans survived the onslaught, but Santa Anna had them killed, as well. As if the passions of the people of Texas weren't inflamed enough, Santa Anna then ordered the execution of 330 prisoners at Goliad on March 27.

As many settlers were *"flying for their lives"*, and Texan forces were compelled to fall back, the Mexican army began to taste victory. However, in the Battle of San Jacinto on April 21, Texan General Sam Houston planned to show the Mexicans that they had bitten off more then they could chew. In a bold surprise attack, 800 Texans overwhelmed 1500 Mexicans in only twenty minutes. The infamous Santa Anna was captured during the battle, but was released after granting Texas its desired independence.

It is interesting to note, however, that for all its protestations about freedom and independence, Texas, like the American colonies before it, held slaves. The slavery issue delayed Texas' entrance into the Union until 1845, an act which began the Mexican War. Santa Anna was again defeated by American forces during this war; forces whose skills were honed for a future conflict, one unlike any other the world had seen. During that conflict, the slave-owning state of Texas once again took up arms, this time against the same Union it had struggled for so long to join.

Thompson's nephew would not only go on to uphold the family's ideals, he would carry them to a new dimension; as a clergyman he would devote his life to the welfare of others, especially in aiding the wounded during the Civil War.

Unfortunately, despite whatever virtues the Thompson family espoused, war was an almost constant reality which had to be faced in realistic and concrete terms. Thompson may have wished for peace, but he wouldn't hesitate to *"belt on my loaded pistols"* in response to danger. The dangerous situation about which he wrote in 1836 was Texas' struggle for independence from Mexico. However, what Thompson apparently didn't yet know on April 28, 1836, was that a week earlier, the Texans had defeated the Mexican forces at the Battle of San Jancinto and won their independence. But even as the flames of war were quenched in Texas, sparks were igniting yet another conflict in Florida.

The trouble actually began two decades earlier. The Creek Indians had been forced to relinquish large tracts of land in the Southeast to the United States after being defeated by the army in 1814. However, one branch of the Creeks, the Seminoles, would not submit. The independence-minded Seminoles moved south into Florida and made new homes and governed themselves. This infuriated the settlers and rich land owners, who became further incensed when they learned that these same Indians were welcoming with open arms, any slaves who escaped their white masters. These two intolerable factors, combined with the obvious fact that Florida was owned by the Spanish and the United States wanted it, prompted the first Seminole War, fought between 1816-1818.

All Is Not Fair

They mean to hold a council on the 18th Inst at Fort Dade, with all the Seminole Chiefs - and it is believed that this would terminate the war, which desirable object I pray may be accomplished.

Mary Thompson passed along this news to an aquaintance in February, 1837, and was referring to negotiations for peace in the second Seminole War. If the council did take place on February 18, its results were ineffective. However, rather dramatic results were obtained during a meeting on October 21, at Fort Peyton.

As the saying goes, "All is fair in love and war", but in peace negotiations there must be rules. General Jesup of the United States Army not only bent those rules in October of 1837, he completely shattered them. Jesup sent a member of his staff, General Hernandez, to arrange a meeting with the great Seminole Chief Osceola under a flag of truce at Fort Peyton. Osceola agreed and he and his men (among whom were ex-slaves) were formally escorted to the fort in full ceremonial dress.

Once inside the fort, as a sign of good faith, the Seminoles put down their weapons with dignity and ceremony. In response, the instant they were disarmed, soldiers took them into custody in an act of treachery that even disgusted the soldiers, themselves. "I shall never forget that day nor the faces of Chief Osceola and the other Indians," one of the soldiers wrote. "We were outraged by the cowardly way he was betrayed into capture."

Newspapers in Washington and New England declared that the capture of Osceola was a shameful act which would justifiably breed distrust among native American peoples. Unfortunately, even if public opinion had called for Osceola's release, it would soon have been a lost cause; the Indian Chief died in prison in 1838. Yet as despicable as the Osceola affair was, it paled in comparison to an event which had occurred in July, 1816.

The overriding reason for the first of the three Seminole Wars was the fact that runaway slaves were living happily in Florida, which was owned by Spain. Georgia land-owners were enraged at the thought of their "property" daring to live like human beings. To make matters worse, these ex-slaves were living peacefully with the Indians. The U.S. Army decided to take action against this outrage (and possibly take over Florida along the way). Their main target was Negro Fort on the Apalachicola River.

The fort had been occupied by the British during the War of 1812 and when they left after the war, possession was turned over to the ex-slaves and Indians who renamed it Negro Fort. To the inhabitants, the fort and the rich farmlands surrounding it symbolized the achievement of their dreams. To Americans, it was an intolerable insult to their way of life; an insult which must be answered with swift and certain justice.

Late in July, 1816, that justice came in the form of U.S. gunboats trespassing into Spanish territory with the sole purpose of bombarding the men, women and children of Negro Fort. When ordinary shot seemed ineffective against the thick, earthen walls, the cannon balls were heated and the first, glowing-red shot scored a direct hit on the fort's powder magazine. The resulting explosion instantly obliterated entire families as everyone in the fort was either killed or severely wounded. The 332 casualties and total destruction of Negro Fort was looked upon favorably by the Southern slave owners who undoubtedly felt that it if they couldn't have their slaves back, killing them all was the next best thing.

American forces led by Andrew Jackson defeated the Indians, and Spain finally relinquished Florida to the United States in 1819. Unfortunately for the Seminoles, the first war was only the beginning of their problems. As settlers once again streamed into new territory, the age-old American problem once again reared its ugly head; Indians lived on fertile land, white settlers wanted fertile land, Indians had to go.

Before engaging in a full-scale, costly war, the government sought a more expeditious and economical way of ridding Florida of its Indian impediments. They offered to trade the lush lands of Florida, teeming with fruits, fish and game, for land in Oklahoma. Some Seminoles knew the consequences of refusing the offer and decided it was better to be alive in Oklahoma, than dead in Florida. But others steadfastly refused to leave their homes and the second Seminole War began in 1835.

It was a bloody beginning. At the end of December, 1835, Major Dade left Fort Brooke at Tampa Bay and headed for Fort Drane, approximately an eight-day march to the northeast. Four days into the trip, all of Major Dade's 112 men were killed in a surprise attack. On that same day, December 28, Seminole Chief Osceola led another surprise attack on General Thompson (no known relation to Major Thompson) at Fort King. During negotiations before the war, General Thompson had imprisoned Osceola and put him in chains, an offense for which the General paid by receiving fifteen Indian bullets and losing his scalp.

The government was determined to bring swift retribution against the Seminoles, but a force led by General Winfield Scott quickly discovered that it would not be that simple. Unlike past wars with European adversaries, where the opposing sides obligingly lined up and fired at one another, the Seminoles were masters of a new tactic; guerrilla warfare. Concealed among the hammocks and swamps, the Indians taught the Americans that despite being outnumbered, an enemy can't be killed if they can't be found. Scott wrote to Secretary of War Lewis Cass and declared that if they were to win the war, no less than three thousand troops were necessary.

General Winfield Scott (1786-1866) was
a leading military figure for 50 years, and
a friend of the Thompson family.

As part of the ensuing increase of manpower, Major Alexander Ramsay Thompson found himself at Tampa Bay by January of 1837 [47]. The move prompted Mrs. Thompson in New York City to spring to action; letter-writing action. While it isn't clear who wore the pants in the Thompson household, it is certain who wielded the pen.

The following series of letters reads like a Who's Who of the military as she uses all of her connections, and talent for words, to try to bring her husband home.

---

[47] It may have been by late 1836. January 27, 1837 is the first record of his being at that location.

To General Winfield Scott from Mary Thompson, New York City, February 21, 1837:

General,

As I understand Colonel Cutler is shortly to be relieved as Superintendent of the Recruiting Service of the Eastern Department, I take the liberty of Soliciting your influence in obtaining for Maj Thompson that Situation for the next term.

For the last three years we have led a roving and unsettled life, having been Stationed at no one place for any length of time; a great portion of which Major T has been compelled to be Separated from his immediate family. From last April until Dec, he was doing arduous duty on that 'harassing Campaign' on the So. W. Border; at present he is in Florida, and for the last year I may Say has been on Continued dayly fatigue -

Add to this, the fact, that his aged mother, who has been dangerously ill; is at present in very feeble health...She is extremely desirous of having her Son near her for a little while ere She goes to her final home.

I trust therefore General, that you will pardon me for intruding upon you at this moment, and in asking an interest in those benevolent feelings of your heart, which you have always wished toward our family -

Should you obtain for the Major this desirable location you will place me under the most mighty obligation to your friendship, and add to this our high estimation I have always held for your Character both as a Soldier and a Gentleman -

> *Written with Sentiments of Great Esteem*
> *I have the Honor to be*
> *Your Most Obedient Servant*
> *Mary W Thompson*

To Brigadier General Jones, Adjutant General, U.S. Army, Washington, D.C., from Mary Thompson, New York City, March, 1837:

General

Having recently understood that Col Cutler will be relieved as Sup. of the Rec. Service of the W. Dept. - I take the liberty to Solicit the particular favor, that Maj T may be appointed to fill the vacancy...

...He is now in Florida, and I feel extremely anxious, if it can be consistent within propriety and duty , that he may by the above appointment receive a little relaxation, from those Severe exposures which have already greatly affected his Constitution -

I would not ask any thing General, that is improper or unreasonable but I have ventured to express my wishes to you without his knowledge & trust that the benevolence of your heart will make allowance for the deep solitude I feel, & which has induced me to address you on this Subject...

When that position didn't appear available, Mary tried a different approach; one in which she didn't hesitate to inform on another officer.

To Major Stewart, Washington, D.C., from Mary Thompson, New York City, July 1, 1837:

Dear Major,

I hope you will excuse my taking the liberty of asking your friendly aid in obtaining a furlough for Major Thompson. - He has made application for one, thru General Jesup, who has approved of, and forwarded it - I am apprehensive however that the Major will not be able to leave Florida until relieved by a Field Officer - Lt Colonel Bliss I understand is on furlough 'til September, and intends, if possible to Keep out of Florida - But I trust he will not be permitted to...

To Major General Alexander Macomb, Washington, D.C., from Mary Thompson, New York City, July 20, 1837:

General

Important business affairs have for some time past, required the presence of Maj Thompson, and which, if much longer neglected may in future cause us much inconvenience & embarrassment -

I therefore take the liberty to address you Sir, as an efficient friend who can aid in this present situation.

I had flattered myself that I would have the pleasure of my Husbands return after a Campaign of duty in the field for more than 16 months; when Lt Col Bliss should join in September - but having understood that it is the intention of Col B. not to join the Hd Qr of his Regt which is in Florida, if he can possibly avoid it: I beg leave Respectfully to Solicit your friendly interference, & allow Maj T to come on in September - at the expiration of Col B. furlough -

I would not Sir, upon any consideration, interfere with any arrangements emanating from the W. Dept. concerned with the good of the Service: my long connection with the army & sense of propriety would forbid such an effort: But I am confident Genl, that your own Kind feelings will properly appreciate the motives which induce the present communication...

P.S. I would remark General, that this letter is my own act, unauthorized by Maj T. - and only designed to assist his furlough, for which I have been informed he has applied.
                                                                                        MWT

   It is clear that Mary Thompson's "*long connection with the army*" taught her that the only way to get what she wanted was to "*interfere*"; with Generals, the War Department or anyone else who might be able to help her. With so many friends in high places, it is curious that Major Thompson did not receive a position back in New York.

Of course, the answer could simply be that he did not want to go to New York while his country was at war in Florida and his regiment was in the thick of it. Perhaps Mary's letters were "*unauthorized by Major T*", because she knew that her husband would be reluctant to leave his men.

Regardless of the situation, no one could blame Mary Thompson for wanting Major Thompson at home; not after two decades of living a "*roving life*", and especially not after hearing the following news from her husband in Florida:

...Letters from the Major of the 7th Inst [February] *informs that the indians & scouts took 4 scalps, among which was a Seminole Chief named Cooper who commanded the Negroes - they also took 1000 head of Cattle, Some Negroes & about 200 indian horses & ponies - Some of which were ready packed for the March - together with a number of women and children...*

Reports from Florida continued to be chilling; Indians seemed to appear out of nowhere to burn settlements and slaughter the inhabitants. Of course, in defense of the Seminoles, they simply wanted to protect their homes and allow runaway slaves the opportunity to live in freedom. It was a difficult war for a man of conscience and although Major Thompson knew his duty, he did confess that he could sympathize with the Seminoles and understood why they didn't want to leave their beautiful homelands.

When September arrived, Major Thompson received neither his furlough, nor a position in the Recruiting Service. What he did receive was something which he probably felt was even better; on September 6, 1837, he was promoted to the rank of Lieutenant Colonel of the 6th Infantry, the Infantry in which he began his career after graduating from West Point. However, if news of her husband's promotion had lifted Mary's spirits, its effects were not long-lasting. When October arrived, Mary Thompson was sick from anxiety and fearful that she would never again she her husband alive.

To Mrs. Winfield Scott at Hampton Place, Elizabethtown, New Jersey, from Mary Thompson, 415 Washington Street, New York City, October 2, 1837:

My Dear Madam,

...I am now on the <u>Sick report</u>, and have been for some time, being under the physician's care, who has prohibited me from using undue exercise or fatigue, as my disease has some connection with the <u>Heart</u> , and therefore urging great attention.

I wish if possible, to make a short visit to West Point, before the Cold Weather sets in, but the Doctor has bid me 'wait orders,'

I am Still denied the gratification of my Husband's return, and despair of Seeing him, 'til this wretched war is over, if indeed it is ever to come to a close, My anxieties on this Subject, no doubt have a great effect upon my general health, and it is impossible for me to struggle effectually against - Tho' it is my continual effort, to try and commit all my anxieties to Him, who is the only Helper of those who truly trust in Him - and trust He will impart to me the grace of patience and Submission -

Mama Thompson has spent a few days here, and returned to West Point - she sends her best love to you, and bids me Say, that She would gladly have made you a Short visit, but the continued delicate State of her health, and the imperative call of duties at Home[48], would not admit of her making a longer journey this time. She hopes, with myself, to be able to do so at a future period.

Be pleased to remember me affectionately to my young friends, Cornelia and Adeline - and a Kiss for the little pet.

Hoping My Dear Mrs Scott, that you may Soon be permitted to enjoy the pleasure of the Generals Society in his speedy return -

I am,

truly and Affectionately
Yours
Mary W. Thompson

On Christmas Day, 1837, Mary's greatest fear was realized; Lieutenant Colonel Alexander Ramsay Thompson was killed at the Battle of Okeechobee. The following is a description of the fatal battle:

...Colonel [Zachary] Taylor, who had been efficiently operating there since its commencement, succeeded in bringing a large party of Indians to an engagement near Okee-Chobee lake. They were posted in swamps and forests close to the water, and fired upon the Americans as they approached. Although the latter were fatigued by long marches, the colonel ordered an immediate charge, which was gallantly performed, through water knee deep, and in face of galling fire. On reaching the opposite bank a desperate battle ensued, which lasted three hours with heavy loss on both sides. It resulted in the total overthrow of the Indians, who were driven from their position by the bayonet, and pursued for some miles. The Americans lost twenty-six killed, and one hundred and twelve wounded, including many valuable officers. The Indians were almost annihilated; and this battle was the last in which they appeared in any considerable number.[49]

Among those twenty-six killed was indeed a most valuable officer, Lt. Col. Thompson, who's role in the battle is best expressed in the words of his widow, Mary.

...And never was there more cool deliberation displayed, than on that fatal day, when in front of his Regiment, amidst the deadly fire of the Enemy, in the hottest of the battle, with a ball in each breast, he remained firm and encouraged his men to, "Remember the Regiment to which they belonged". These were the last words he uttered - and his Regiment and Country will never forget them. Thus, he yielded up his life, upon the fatal battle field of Okee-cho-bee, in Florida, on the 25 December, 1837. A pattern of bravery rarely equalled.

---

[48] Most likely the feeding of the cadets at her home.
[49] John Frost, Popular History of the United States, R. Worthington, 1881.

The Battle of Okeechobee, December 25, 1837. Colonel Alexander Ramsay Thompson was killed during the battle after receiving three musket balls in the chest. Though mortally wounded, he calmly continued to lead his men and his last words were, "Remember the Regiment to which you belong!"

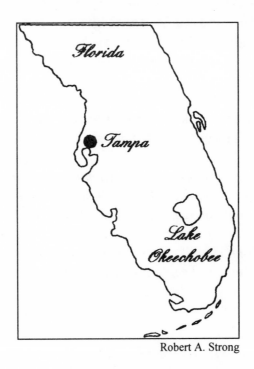

Robert A. Strong

Once again, it might be difficult to believe the words of a grieving widow, but the official army dispatch confirms Colonel Thompson's uncommon bravery.

Although he received two balls from the fire of the enemy early in the action, which wounded him severely, yet he appeared to disregard them, and continued to give his orders with the same coolness that he would have done had his regiment been under review, or any other parade duty. Advancing, he received a third ball, which at once deprived him of life; his last words were, "Keep steady, men; charge the hammock - remember the regiment to which you belong." [50]

Zachary Taylor's (1785-1850) bold actions in the army earned him the nickname "*Old Rough and Ready*". He was in command at the Battle of Okeechobee and personally wrote of Thompson's bravery. Taylor became the 12th President of the United States in 1848, but died of cholera after only 16 months in offfice.

The heroic death of Lt. Col. Alexander Ramsay Thompson is truly an instance where "*no picture of imagination*" could surpass "*in wonder the realities of life*"; a work of fiction could not have created a more gallant and courageous death. And as Thompson had asked his men to remember their regiment, so the regiment remembered Thompson; his bravery was not forgotten, not by his men and not by the Military Academy at West Point, from which he had graduated.

On May 25, 1838, funeral services were held at the Academy's chapel. The services were conducted by Isaac Ferris, D.D., who almost thirty years later as Chancellor of the University of the City of New York, would confer the degree of Doctor of Divinty to Thompson's nephew, Alexander, the boy Thompson hoped would follow the path of "*Virtue & Integrity*". A tall monument was erected in the West Point cemetery as the Colonel's remains were laid to rest just a few feet away from his father's. The inscription around the base encapsulates the Colonel's life, and death.

---

[50] Cullum.

SACRED TO THE REMAINS
OF
LT. COL. ALEX. R. THOMPSON
U. STATES 6TH INFANTRY
BORN FEB. 19, 1793. FELL DEC. 25 1837.
AT THE HEAD OF HIS REGIMENT,
IN A SUCCESSFUL CHARGE
BATTLE OF OKEE-CHO-BEE,
FLORIDA

THE SON OF A GALLANT OFFICER
OF THE REVOLUTIONARY ARMY
WHOSE REMAINS LIE NEAR THIS SPOT
HIS DEVOTION TO COUNTRY
WAS THE DICTATE
OF PRINCIPLE & EXAMPLE

THIS MONUMENT
IS THE JOINT TRIBUTE
OF HIS AFFECTIONATE WIDOW
AND ADMIRING REGIMENT

WITH MORALS
FOUNDED ON CHRISTIAN PIETY
HIS LIFE WAS AS EXEMPLARY
AS HIS DEATH WAS GLORIOUS

While the memory of Colonel Thompson was crowned in glory, his widow, Mary, had to face the stark realities of survival. That survival was dependent upon money and she quickly set about trying to obtain her widow's pension. Once again, the documents in the Ricca Collection show Mary's talent for writing; her pen appears to have at least been as mighty as her husband's sword.

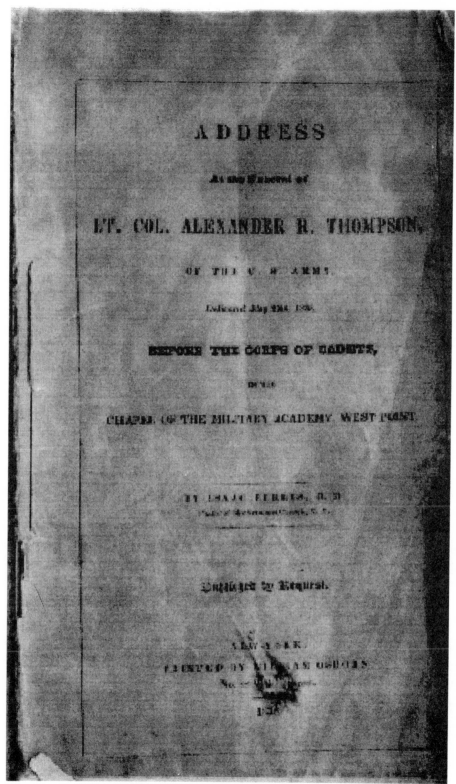

The cover of the program for the funeral service held for Colonel Thompson
at the chapel of the United States Military Academy, May 25, 1838.

To the <u>Honorable, the Senate</u>, and <u>House of Representatives</u> of the United States, in Congress assembled.

The <u>Memorial of Mary W. Thompson</u>,
Widow of the late <u>Lt</u>. <u>Colonel Alexander Ramsay Thompson</u>, of the United States Army, respectfully sheweth

That having been placed by the Divine Providence in a condition that renders it necessary for her to make application to Government for relief, she begs leave to present her case in such an aspect, as to exhibit the propriety and justice of her claim; and there-by induce your Honorable Body, so as to favor it, that the result shall be her obtaining the aid she thus so earnestly solicits.

My deceased lamented Husband, was the son of the late Captian Alexander Thompson, of the United States Army, who was a Revolutionary Officer, having engaged in that Service, at the age of sixteen years; and, passed with Honor and Reputation through that memorable and sanguinary struggle, which gained for us as a Nation, Liberty and Independence. His son, the late Lt Colonel Alexander R. Thompson, also entered the, Service, as a Cadet, at the Military Academy, West Point, in the year 1810, with a firm determination to devote his Life to the service and interests of his Country.

At the commencement of the war in 1812, he was appointed a Lieutenant in the Army and ordered to the North. He was at the Seige of Plattsburgh, and tho' but a youth, in many instances Honorably distinguisbed himself in command of 100 men he gallantly defended a bridge, which the enemy was endeavouring to pass. His Military skill and correct deportment, gained for him a character of science. intrepidity and cool deliberation (qualities which he truly possessed) and which bore him through the many trying situations in which be has been placed; and which he so affectingly exemplified in the disastrous Battle, wherein he generously and nobly yielded up his Life, in devotion to the interests of his Country -- and to the Honor of this service, which was so closely interwoven with the best feelings of his heart.

Your Memorialist, would further most respectfully state, to the Honorable Senate, and to the House of Representatives, that my lamented Husbands' services, during the period of Twenty five Years, have been unremitted. He has served at every Military Post in the Northern Frontier and on the Western, and South Western Border. He has planned and erected many of our Forts and buildings, employing his whole time in such practical duties - supervising works - making improvements - disbursing monies in the erection of Public buildings - and settling private claims on lands occupied by Government.

He has surveyed, and made reservations; for selected sites for Light Houses: opened Roads, erected bridges, and performed (without compensation) every duty that could have been performed by a Military Officer; Agent of Indian Affairs, or a General Agent for the Government, as papers in my possession confirm.

Colonel Thompson, has also been the Military Instructor of the Troops at every station where he has been placed. He was the Moral as well as the Military pattern for the Youthful Officer, and soldier of his command.

In the year 1820, when in command of the 2nd Infantry, it was reviewed by the Honorable John C. Calhoun, and by him pronouinced to be the best specimen of American Infantry he had ever witnessed. Colonel Thompson devoted himself to make the troops under his command, efficient for any service, of which his last Battle is an evidence, and which has confirmed for our Army, its exalted reputation; and for which every surviving officer (I believe) has justly received distinguished Honors.

Your Memorialist, further states that the last two years of the life Lt Colonel Thompson were passed in Campaigns - one, on the Mexican Border, and one in Florida; during which time he performed the duties of a Brigadier and Major General; while he only received the pay of a Major of Infantry. Suffering much privation, loss of Health and enduring great hardship and fatigue - (yet, notwithstanding he never relinquished his command, nor suffered himself to be placed on the sick report. When the Campaign under Colonel (now Genl) Taylor commenced its march from Tampa, he was urged to remain, being considered too much enfeebled in health to under take the march - but he absolutely refused, stating that he could not consent to remain absent from his Regiment, and that he would not give up as long as be could keep his seat in saddle.

And never was there more cool deliberation displayed, than on that fatal day, when in the front of his Regiment, amidst the deadly fire of the Enemy, in the hottest of the battle, with a ball in each breast, be remained firm and encouraged his men, to, "Remember the Regiment to which they belonged". These were the last words he uttered - and his Regiment and Country will never forget them. Thus, he yielded up his life, upon the fatal battle field of Okee-cho-bee, in Florida, on the 25 December 1837. A pattern of bravery rarely equalled.

The constant changes to which we were subjected for the last twelve years, rendered many expences unavoidable and the sacrifice and loss of furniture, inevitable. And made it impracticable for us to raise a fund for future support, in such a case as I now realize. Even the late changes, which ordered us to Louisiana, and from there to Florida, destroyed all our effects by mildew, damps and other means, with the exception of Colonel Thompsons' Uniform - when these things were received in New York, the most of them were so injured, as to be useless.

Your Memorialist, I would most Respectfully represent to the Honorable the Senate, and to the House of Representatives - that she has patiently and cheerfully accompanied her beloved Husband, the late Lt Colonel Thompson, thru' all his travels, (in Florida excepted) for 22 years; not to hinder him in his duty, but to help and cheer him on in its faithful performance; she has evinced and proved her attachment to her late husband, and also her aspect and Admiration for that Gallant Army of which he was a Member. This feeling, so faithfully cherished during his life. Now, that he sleeps in the Grave of Honor, she desires to cherish for his memory, and she does not deem it derogatory, but perfectly proper to solicit and receive from Government, that aid which it is in its power to bestow. That respectably, and independently she may pass the remainder of her life, free from those anxieties, which would otherwise agitate it.

Your Memorialist, under a high apprehension of the liberality for which the Honorable the Senate, and the House of Representatives, are eminently distinguished in every just cause, in the Confidence of Hope; and in an anticipation of this kind Consideration in which they will view this Memorial, so Mournfully induced. Also, of the

Honorable the Senate, and the House of Representatives, to pass a Law, granting her an annuity of full pay for life, under the same restrictions, as are contained in the present law, granting half pay to the Widows of Officers Killed in Battle - or an Equivalent.

For all of Mary Thompson's eloquence, she did not receive the full-pay-for-life pension she sought, but the half-pay pension for five years which was the standard policy. To even qualify for that, there were papers to be filed, petitions to be written and records to be verified, every six months of the five-year term. However, Mary was not content with the standard pension and continued to fight for additional money for the next twenty years, although her pleas seldom reached sympathetic ears.

In a letter to her brother-in-law, William, she describes her difficulties with the government in terms which could easily be read as a reaction to any number of present-day complaints.

Dear William,   *Washington, D.C.*
                                                                   March 6. 1840

...I do not hesitate to Say, this is the most disgraceful Congress that ever sat - They Seem determined not to allow a Single Claim, whether just or not - and try to prevent a dollar from being appropriated - <u>except</u> to pamper their own prodigal extravagances for themselves - and they will Sit and Squander thousands of money - on their outrageous speeches to Send throughout the Country - for the purpose of Electioneering - and the <u>Small</u> sum of $100,000 is appropriated for the Stationery & printing of the House, besides $400,000 for the pay of these <u>noble liberal minded men</u> - and $25,000 for the Clerks of the House & $25,000 for the Stationery & printing of the Senate - and yet they pause and hesitate at allowing a Single farthing for the 20 or 30 years faithful Service of an officer of the Army - whose life has been yielded up for them - and they close their ears to the prayer of the widow & the orphan[51] who ask a pitance justly due - I am sick at heart & discouraged...

Mary Thompson may have been down, but she was never out. She continued writing to government officials and politicians of all levels of importance and influence; one lenghty letter from 1853 was even sent to the Secretary of War, Mr. Jefferson Davis, future President of the Confederate States of America. Mary's attack was three-pronged: 1. Attempting to obtain a full-pay pension for life. 2. Attempting to obtain compensation for duties her husband had performed throughout his military career which were above and beyond the scope of his rank. 3. Attempting to obtain compensation for illnesses and injuries Colonel Thompson had received in the line of duty.

Mary met with limited success with the last two requests, but the full-pay pension continued to elude her. Once again, however, she was not above naming names in an attempt to get what she wanted.

---

[51] Although Mary makes mention several times of "*an orphan nephew to provide for*", neither the name of the parents or of the child is recorded.

Undated letter, possibly to Senator Thomas Benton:

...I cannot conceive, why the widow of an officer of my Husbands rank - He falling under the circumstances he did - on the field of battle - at the head of his Reg - & in the <u>prime of life</u> - should be put on the pension list at so low an estimate - when other Widows, whose Husbands have died naturally and at Home, should receive full half pensions agreeing with the rank of their husbands - Many of whom now are receiving them for life. I understand that the widow of Col Fowle, whose promotion was occasioned by the fall of mine - & when on the way to join his Reg - was blown up on a Steam Boat on the Ohio - receives ample pension for life - Mrs. McNeil, Mrs. McCrea, Mrs. Hoffman & others - all of whose Husbands - with the exception of Col Fowle, died natural Deaths - they are receiving pensions for life - as my health is very precarious and the allotted period of human existence fast approaching its close - leaving me but few years in number - The very limited & uncertain income arising from what little property I possess giving me no adequate support - The certainty of a sum derived from a pension would relieve my mind from much anxiety, & and contribute much to my comfort...

The government was not the only resource Mary attempted to tap, nor the only area in which she flexed her business muscle.

To Mary's brother Elias Nexsen, from Washington, February 15, 1843:

On the 2nd Inst. I wrote to you and enclosed a draft for $100...I am certain you would not willingly cause me any uneasiness - but when I send money, I want it acknowledged - You know , promptitude in business is my motto - & especially in the acknowledgement of money transmitted this ought to be observed...

To Michael (Doushaw?) from Mary Thompson in Washington, February 20, 1843:

In looking over some of the papers of my lamented Husband a short time since, I found a receipt given by yourself for 3 Horses belonging to Colonel Thompson, which you "agree to Keep for him until called for in consideration of the services they may render you".
Will you have the goodness to inform me whether these horses are still in your possession - or if not, what has become of them or what disposition has been made of them.
The above receipt you gave on the departure of Col Thompson from Mackinac in 1833...an early answer will oblige me...

To William (Weir?), Michigan from Mary Thompson, Washington, February, 1843:

You say you are anxious to purchase 80 acres of land, shortly to be sold by the heirs of Col Cummings, & the price will probably be 2.50 per acre...I think it <u>high</u> at 2.50 - you can buy Govt land at 1.25 - probably as good as this...

Mary Thompson continued to fight for additional money[52] well into her 60's. In fact, she probably kept fighting until the day she died, which was June 8, 1858. She was buried next to her husband in the cemetery at West Point, her grave marker simply reading:

Mary Waldron Nexsen
Relict of
Lt. Col. Alex. R. Thompson
Born Feb. 24, 1790
Died June 8, 1858

Had Mary Thompson survived a few more years, she would have witnessed yet another war, but a war unlike any other she had known. It would be up to her nephew, Alexander, to carry the Thompson legacy into a new era. And while the next Alexander Thompson would also serve his coutry with unwavering devotion, he would choose to take his orders from a power higher than the United States Army and as his uncle had advised, would *"let the Bible be his book of regulations"*.

---

[52] Mary also attempted to obtain a land grant as the widow of an officer based upon an Act of Congress passed September 28, 1850.

Chapter 3

"These are the times..."

Reverend Alexander Ramsay Thompson, 1822-1895.

When Reverend Alexander Ramsay Thompson was born on October 16, 1822, he came into a family which had two very strong characteristics; a love of country and a devotion to religion. For the two generations of Alexander Thompsons who preceded him, these characteristics blended to create military men of honor, integrity and conscience. The third Alexander possessed all of these qualities, but he chose to express them in the role of a clergyman, even though he, too, possessed that same *"soldier blood"* which *"nerved his will, inspired his loyalty"* and *"stirred him vehemently when face to face with wrong."*[53]

This *"soldier blood"* descended to him from both sides of his family. On his father's side was his uncle, Colonel Thompson, who was a veteran of the War of 1812 and died in the second Seminole War. His grandfather, Captain Thompson, was a veteran of the Revolutionary War and also spent his life in the service of his country. Alexander's mother, Janette Nexsen, was the daughter of Elias Nexsen, who was also an officer during the Revolutionary War. While he was proud of this heritage, his course in life was decided upon as a child, and perhaps was foreshadowed by the place of his birth.

In 1822, another yellow fever epidemic was ravaging New York City. In order to protect his family, William Robert Thompson brought his daughters and pregnant wife to the home of a friend in Bloomingdale, New York. That friend happened to be Reverend Alexander Gunn and his home was the parsonage of the Bloomingdale Church, where Alexander Ramsay Thompson was born. Alexander would have no brothers[54], but he would have six sisters, two of whom died very young. There is no mention of any financial difficulties for the large family, as William Thompson's drug store must have provided them a comfortable living.

The Thompsons were at least secure enough financially to send young Alexander to a private school in Newburgh, New York, where at the age of ten, he began his education with Reverend M. Phinney. He appears to have been an exceptional student, and he entered college at the age of fourteen. The same year his uncle was killed in the Battle of Okeechobee, Alexander was a freshman at New York University. After spending a year working at his father's store and attending Rutgers University during his sophomore year, he returned to N.Y.U. where he graduated in June, 1842.

If there were any doubts as to his chosen profession, the records do not indicate it; two months after graduating, Alexander Ramsay Thompson entered the Theological

---

[53] From Reverend Alexander Ramsay Thompson's obituary written by Reverend Joseph Duryre which appeared in the <u>Christian Intelligencer</u>, February 20, 1895.

[54] Thompson's obituary states that late in life *"brothers, sisters, and lifelong friends quickly passed away"*, but in Thompson's own family history he listed no brothers.

Seminary at Princeton in New Jersey, where he remained for the next three years. The year 1845 was to be eventful for the young man. On March 15 of that year, he was licensed to preach by the Second Presbyterian Church of New York. In May, he graduated from the Theological Seminary. In July, he became the assistant to Reverend Broadhead in a church in Brooklyn, New York. Finally, to complete the whirlwind year, Alexander became engaged to Mary Carpenter, the sister of Dr. Hugh Carpenter, one of his classmates from N.Y.U., and the daughter of a prominent New York physician, Dr. John Carpenter.

Reverend Alexander Ramsay Thompson was ordained on January 16, 1846 and his first ministry was at the First Presbyterian Church in Morristown, New Jersey, where he and Mary were married in October of that year. It is interesting to note that in a family with so many similar names, they shared other things in common as well; Alexander's grandfather, Captain Thompson, was also married in Morristown[55] to Amelia De Hart, who was also the daughter of a physician.

For the next fifteen years, Reverend Thompson and his growing family moved every few years as he obtained different positions in various churches. Fortunately, however, these moves did not entail death-defying journeys across wild frontiers. These travels were taken through the streets and rolling farmlands of Brooklyn and Staten Island, New York. From 1848 to 1859, Reverend Thompson was on Staten Island where he developed many life-long friendships and where he probably gave every indication of spending the rest of his days in the quiet life of a country preacher. But that quiet life would end for him, and for the nation, during his next ministry in Bridgeport, Connecticut.

On March 1, 1859, Reverend Thompson became pastor of the South Church in Bridgeport. The church was also known as the Second Congregational Church, because in 1830, disagreements among the members of the First Congregational Church led to a congregational secession and the South Church was formed.[56] However, there still seems to have been some dissent among the members of the South Church and Thompson's years there were not easy. Still, his devotion to his duty, though tested, did not waver and two fruits of his labor were missionary schools he organized. One was in East Bridgeport, which led to the formation of another Congregational Church and the other was for the black children in a section of town known as "Liberia".

In the fall of 1860, construction on a new South Church began across the street from the old church at the corner of Broad and Gilbert Streets, only a block away from its estranged sister church of the First Congregation. Unfortunately, a new church building did not cure the spiritual ills of its members. Early in 1861, Thompson would write about the "*spiritual collapse*" of his congregation and how his "*soul was utterly at sea*". Whatever the nature of this "*spiritual collapse*" was, it caused Thompson to confess that he "*never felt more utterly helpless*" and that it was "*hard to fight away a feeling of contempt for some of these people*".

---

[55] They were married on March 4, 1784.
[56] The two churches would merge again in 1916.

The South Church, which stood at the corner of Broad and Gilbert Streets in Bridgeport, Connecticut, was constructed in 1860-61, while Reverend Thompson was its minister.

The Greatest Showman on Earth

August 31, 1861 diary entry of Reverend Thompson:

Went to Barnum's Museum to see the Hippopotamus with which I was a good deal interested.

Reverend Thompson befriended many interesting people throughout his life, but arguably, the most interesting was Phineas T. Barnum. While the two men enjoyed their witty and stimulating conversation, the devout minister and the blustering showman must have made a very odd couple.

> Rev. Mr. Thompson being called for arose amid great applause, but excused himself from speaking on account of fatigue from the labors of the day. He and Mr. Barnum had a tilt at wit which created great good humor in the audience. The Rev. gentleman agreed to speak five minutes, which time he employed in a characteristic speech.

Article in the *Bridgeport Evening Standard*, February 24, 1861.

Barnum became famous for his outrageous marketing abilities, although there was not always truth in his advertising. In 1835, he put an old woman on display, billing her as George Washington's nurse when he was a child (Washington was born in 1732). Occasionally, even when he was honest, he wasn't believed. The term "white elephant" arose from a genuine white elephant which Barnum exhibited, but everyone believed was a fake. Barnum's showmanship even added a new word to our dictionaries; "Jumbo", after the name of a huge elephant he displayed in 1882.

In addition to beginning his circus, unabashedly called *The Greatest Show on Earth,* in 1871, P.T. Barnum gained worldwide renown for bringing Charles S. Stratton to London for an audience with Queen Victoria. Stratton's popularity was due to his extraordinary height, or lack of it, and Barnum changed the midget's name to General Tom Thumb. He also sponsored the American tour of the wildly popular "Swedish Nightingale", Jenny Lind.

While Barnum's fame and fortunes had their ups and downs during his life, he did leave his indelible mark on American society. Every time one is forced to endure another media blitz about an actor, a product or anything else, remember that it is all a legacy of the Father of Overstatement, P.T. Barnum.

These deep feelings Thompson expressed were not put down on paper for his friends or relatives to read; they were written to himself in a diary he began on January 1, 1861, with the words, *"This book must reproduce my heart."* The diary does indeed reproduce the innermost feelings of his heart, and deepest thoughts of his mind, and because of that it is arguably the most valuable piece in the Ricca Collection for the insight it provides.

The cover of Reverend Thompson's diary.

Reverend Thompson's diary confirms that the public persona of a compassionate, humble clergyman was not merely a facade. He writes openly and honestly about his hopes, fears, doubts and heartfelt desire for the good of all. Numerous letters in the collection speak of the great power of Thompson's words and the diary also reveals that his sermons were inspiring because he personally experienced and understood despair, illness and the pain of losing a loved one, yet endured all of life's tragedies without losing his faith.

It is clear that the cornerstone of Thompson's character and that which motivated all of his actions was his pure, unshakable faith. When his congregation seemed to turn against him, he had faith that his path would be made clear. When he was penniless and his children needed medicine, he had faith that support would be provided. When a terrible illness overcame one of his own children, he had faith that the boy had found comfort in heaven.

That boy was Thompson's beloved infant son, Hugh, and some of the most revealing and poignant entries in his diary involve the painful struggle for *"sweet Hughey's"* life.

Friday, December 13, 1861:

During the day Hughey sickened & by midnight it became evident that he has the Scarlet fever too.

Saturday, December 14:

The children's sickness absorbs all our thoughts...The boy has it very decidedly & it looks as if even severely. They are very sick.

Monday, December 16:

Allie is very sick & Hughey is alarmingly ill...Once in a while a haunting horror of possible peril for them comes over us...

Tuesday, December 17:

Allie continues very ill. So does precious little Hughey. Minny droops very much. Rob has it lightly & Mag is getting very well. Net begins to have the symptoms of it. Sweet Hughey had a fearful attack. From his head to his feet he is covered with the scarlet eruption of the fever. I have never seen anything like it before...

Wednesday, December 18:

There is no let up in dear Hughey's fever. It rages on with uncontrollable violence. Dear lamb he rallies when he can, and to the familiar songs and stories gives some word of reference, says the last word of the stories or mimics the dog or cow faintly which he used to do so briskly...Not a cry of pain, sore as is his sickness & suffering. The shadows deepen drearily. Last night he had a fearful fight of it. His little throat seems to be almost closed tonsils swollen till they seem to touch & inflammation of the bronchia which makes swallowing an anguish & breathing a pain...

Thursday, December 19:

Sweet Hughey sinks so rapidly that the Doctor has betaken to stimulants & in the face of his violent fever every 20 minutes he has wine & brandy in water & beef tea...quinine & iron. He rallies under it & fights bravely along the darling. But oh this awful struggle for life. Everything else begins to fade away from us. The other dear children are ill, but he precious blessed lamb is in deep waters. We forget whether it is day or night...Oh, will he get thru, Hush, wild heart of agony, by this agony of love understand Christ's love for him.

Friday, December 20:

Our lot of unutterable anguish now is to behold in this precious lamb suffering that we have no power to alleviate...This morning his fever seemed to slacken somewhat and a hope gleam shot through our souls. But it was very soon evident that fearful complications had taken place. His right lung was a good deal congested. The bronchia very much inflamed. A great aggregation of mucous in his throat. The mucous membranes all more or less inflamed. The Dr. was evidently sorely alarmed when he saw him this morning...

Saturday, December 21:

About midnight he gave over fighting with the croup and sank into mere quiet...From the cradle to our arms till weary weary he said "bed" & we laid him down. So between one & two of this morning there his mother on one side of the cradle I on the other, he lifted up his dear sweet eyes & gave us an intense look upward. I knew what was coming then & after took him in my arms. His mother said Oh I wish I could hold him & I said you may but quick if you want him...I went around the cradle with him & laid him in her lap & as I did it he did not breathe again. I thought he would, looked to see him do it, but he did not...in my arms & his mothers lap that very instant, sweet precious blessed darling joyful Hughey...

Wednesday, December 25:

Distributed the gifts to the dear youngsters around Minnie's bed, with an overtone of ache for sweet little Koo [Hugh] whose jubilant merriment this morning we had anticipated with so much pleasure, but never mind he is merrier there with Jesus than we could have made him on Earth.

As traumatic as the year 1861 was personally for Thompson, it paled in comparison to what the nation was undergoing. On January 11, Thompson wrote that every morning, he would "*run down town eager for news from the South*". Very disturbing news from the South did begin to filter through the Bridgeport newspaper office the second week of April. On April 13, he recorded, "*We are all greatly agitated by the news of the bombardment of Fort Sumter today & tonight God grant that what we hear may be exaggerated. God help their beleaguered men for Christ's sake!*"

On April 16, 1861, all hopes were dashed that the news was exaggerated and Thompson painfully recorded, "*that Fort Sumter has been bombarded and compelled to surrender. The President has acknowledged it in a proclamation declaring the Southern states in rebellion and calling for 75,000 men. Volunteers are flying to arms. The war spirit flames like the burst of a volcano. Today completes the 16th year of my ministry.*"

Reverend Thompson went to visit relatives in New York City and on April 20, he recorded in his diary that "*the grand event of yesterday was the departure of the 7th Regiment to Washington*". Thompson fought the enormous crowds and followed the troops along the length of their route through the city, describing the sight of the soldiers as being "*a splendid spectacle not without sadness*". Unlike many of those who burned with the war spirit, Thompson realized all too well that war was not all glory.

On April 20, an even grander event occurred; "*the great Union meeting in Union Square*", which he attended. Traveling to Union Square "*by a 4th Ave car*", he found that *"the mass of people was tremendous"* and later wrote these words to describe the historic moment:

Huge crowds gathered on April 19, 1861, to watch the departure of the 7th New York Regiment for Washington. Reverend Thompson watched the procession with his brother-in-law, Dr. Hugh Carpenter.

Squeezed from stand to stand. Saw a great rush at a house in the square & presently to the multitude frantic with huzzai stepped in the balcony a slender military man. It was Maj Anderson [Commander of Fort Sumter when it was bombarded]. When he left the house I went around the corner, got on a lamp and I had a capital view of him...Stood near the Sumter flag & splinter of its staff lashed to the hand of Washington's statue.

Major Anderson from Fort Sumter appeared in Union Square on April 20, 1861. Reverend Thompson stood near the Sumter flag which was placed on the statue of George Washington.

While the rally was inspiring, there never seemed to have been any doubt about Thompson's involvement on behalf of his country. On April 22, a letter from his wife, Mary, indicated that "*a squad of volunteers start for the war front today & that among them are some of our men who desire very much to see you*". Reverend Thompson's duty was clear, but upon returning to Bridgeport, he not only bestowed spiritual aid to the men already in uniform, he immediately began to focus his efforts toward the formation of additional Connecticut regiments. Unfortunately, his actions alienated many friends and members of the church who didn't share Thompson's patriotic fervor. However, these criticisms did not deter him as he was firmly convinced that "*no man can feel at liberty to remain quietly in his tracks*" when the nation was in such turmoil.

Relying upon the strength of his convictions, and a good measure of his soldier's blood, Thompson poured his energies into his work and was particularly instrumental in the formation of the 17th Regiment of Connecticut Volunteer Infantry, commanded by an acquaintance, Colonel William Noble. Thompson even served as their Chaplain for a year, traveling with them as far south as Baltimore.

During those frightening, confusing and exhilarating first few weeks of the war, passions were running high on every level. Amidst the storms of rhetoric and grandiose speech-making, it is a credit to Thompson's character that he was able to summon up the clarity to describe the nation's plight during those days in a simple, yet insightful way. On April 24, Reverend Thompson wrote, "*These are the times, here are the men, this is the work.*"

For Thompson, his work became his magnificent obsession. Although he was greatly concerned for the welfare of the soldiers and the country, his zeal for his work could not be masked. After arriving back in Bridgeport very late on the night of April 22, he was up early the following morning and spent a hectic day with the troops.

Hurried down town this morning & went into the armory of the Light Guard. A great crowd was there. And the company of volunteers under command of Capt Fitzgibbon were drilling. After being a few moments in the room I was requested to speak to the men & stepped up forward made a few remarks to them. Along with Mr. Benedict I guided them in their march to the cars & went over to New Haven with them. Henry Hoyt goes as Lieut., Horace Hanford as Sergt. & in the ranks were some who had more or less moments relation to us - Marched around New Haven with them to their quarters. Tried to say a word here & there of counsel & cheer. Gave Henry & Horace each a testament & psalms. Made another talk of a few words with them there & prayed with the company.

Had Thompson been ten years younger and without more than half a dozen children, he might have done more than just prayed with the company, he may have joined them. But the situation being as it was, Thompson had to content himself with the role of soldier of the spirit. Many of Thompson's friends did enlist, however, and he always did what he could to help. When his assistant, Alfred, signed up, Thompson *"dashed around town & got him a few little notions that I thought would contribute to his comfort"*. Thompson also wrote that *"Payne, Hubbell & Parker helped me give Alfred a revolver which Mark Hawley said he sold for about cost ($12). Alfreds delight was very great at receiving it for he has been eager to possess one. Went down to the Depot & saw them off. God guard & keep him."*

The general sentiment in the North during the spring of 1861 was that the war would only last a few months and the Union forces would win without much difficulty. This wild optimism would come crashing down to brutal reality on July 21 in Manassas[57], Virginia. So confident were the citizens of Washington, D.C. that their troops would easily whip the rebels, that many men and women traveled out to the site of the battle in carriages to have a picnic and watch the entertaining spectacle. However, with unexpected tenacity (of the likes which earned General Stonewall Jackson his nickname), the Confederate forces not only held their ground, they counterattacked, sending Union troops and citizen spectators running for their lives back to Washington.

Not only had the North sustained a stunning defeat, both sides had suffered combined casualties of 3,500; an incredible one-day total considering that during the eight long years of the Revolutionary War, total casualties for the American forces were not much more than twice that number. On July 22, Thompson expressed in his diary the same disbelief which rocked the nation.

...word had come of a great battle and Wo for us! a defeat & rout. It seemed impossible to believe it. I rushed up to the newspaper office, & found alas every bulletin full of the fearful tidings. I feel as if my heart had frozen dead in me.

---

[57] The battle was also known as First Bull Run. Several battles during the Civil War are known by two names because Union forces named battles for bodies of water, while the Confederates named them for nearby towns.

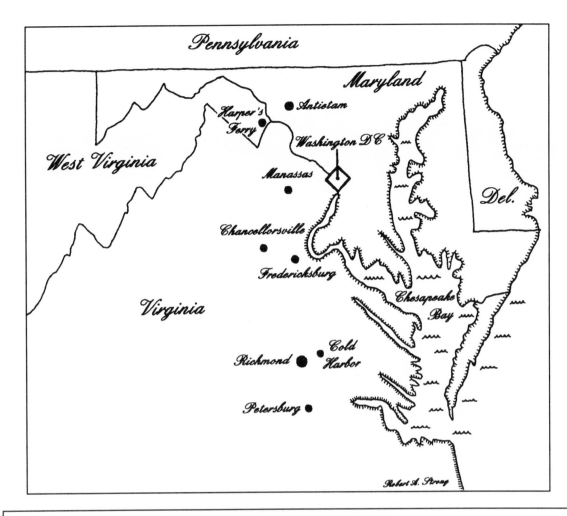

Consecrated in Blood

William Hawley was a friend of Reverend Thompson in Bridgeport, Connecticut. The following letter, dated only *"Sunday P.M."*, is from Hawley and was written during the Civil War, somewhere in Virginia.

I have just come from <u>church</u> & cannot forbear telling you about our new chapel which is just built by the 108th N.Y. of our brigade, with a canvas roof furnished by the Christian Commission, it is the first house we have had the privilege of occupying for religious worship since entering the service - it is built of pine logs, with oaken benches, & plastered in the inside with Virginia mud. Friday it was dedicated to God with prayer & praise, it was ready last Sabbath, but the battle over the river filled it with wounded, doubly precious will the rude house be to us for it is consecrated with the <u>blood</u> of our brave ones, which staining the floors & benches, some of our heroes were brought in then bleeding & mangled, only to be carried out in a short time dead - In this house we who love Jesus hope to have opportunity of celebrating the Lord's Supper, not since July/62 has that dear privilege been mine -

Brave Albion

On August 28, 1861, Reverend Thompson recorded in his diary that he had a visit from Albion Brooks, a young man with a noble character and a pleasant manner. Brooks was also a devout Christian with a strong desire to serve his country; qualities which three generations of Thompsons had admired. Brooks acted upon his desire to serve his country by enlisting with the 8th Connecticut Regiment Volunteer Infantry on November 26, 1861.

On Thanksgiving Day, November 28, 1861, Albion wrote the following to Reverend Thompson:

Burnside Camp Annapolis, Md
My dear Pastor

Here I am a <u>soldier</u> for my country...I have a fine lot of men in my tent...We have a fine Chaplain - he seems to be a true Christian man...Well here it is Thanksgiving & you at home eating Turkey while we poor men are in Dixie with nothing better than hard crackers & "salt horse". Well so be it...I wish I could stand in the Old South Church [Bridgeport] *next Sunday but my duty is here.*

In March of 1862, the 8th Connecticut was first engaged by the enemy at Newberne, North Carolina, and again in April at Fort Macon in that state. On May 28,

Union troops overrunning Confederate defenses at Newberne,
North Carolina, March 14, 1862.

1862, a mutual friend of Albion and Thompson wrote to the Reverend and inquired good-naturedly if he might *"ask brave Albion if his knees did not shake when the shot came whistling around his head*". If Albion's courage had not been tested in the first two engagements, it certainly would have been on September 17, 1862 at the Battle of Antietam, where the 8th CT saw the bloodiest, single day in its history; total casualties for the regiment reached 194 killed, wounded and missing. Total casualties for the Union and Confederate forces that day were over 23,000.

In October of 1862, another mutual friend at Harper's Ferry, West Virginia, wrote to Thompson to inform him that "*Albion Brooks is only about 5 miles from us. I expect a visit from him soon*". That visit may not have taken place as the 8th CT was soon on the move to Fredericksburg, Virginia. In the battle which began on December 13, the 8th CT was not in the thick of things and sustained only three casualties; 1 killed, 2 wounded. Total casualties for the Union at Fredericksburg were over 12,000.

Albion Brooks could have gone home at the end of 1863, but in December, he and over 300 other members of his regiment re-enlisted. After a well-deserved furlough during January-February, 1864, Albion and the 8th CT were back in Virginia. On June 1, 1864, the battle of Cold Harbor began. While casualties were high for the Union (over 6,000 fell in the span of a single hour) the loss for the 8th CT was only 8 killed and 30 wounded. But among those 8 killed, was a special friend of Reverend Thompson; First Sergeant Albion D. Brooks.

Chaplain Moses Smith of the 8th CT Regiment to Reverend Thompson, June 4, 1864:

In an engagement at Cold Harbor June 2d, your dear friend & brother A.D.B. [Albion D. Brooks] was severely wounded. The bullet struck him in the abdomen in the left side & passed through coming out on the other side above the hip. It was supposed that the wound was mortal but we knew that it was safe & would be for his comfort to do all possible. He seemed to rally during the day (he was wounded in the morning) he rested well at night & yesterday morning thought he felt better. I left him for part of the day...on returning found him sinking...At about 1/4 of 9 of last evening, June 3 he quietly breathed his last...A little before his death he said - 'I am going' & then slowly added, 'So I am with You always even unto the end' & soon closed his eyes & breathed more & more slowly...

From Captain William Howe, Head Quarters, 3rd Brigade, 2nd Division, 2nd Army Corps, 14th Connecticut Regiment, to Reverend Thompson, June 7, 1864:

...My chief reason for writing today is to communicate to you the sad news of <u>Albion Brooks</u> death - Learning that the 8th Conn. was in the 18th Corps. which joined the Army of the Potomac recently, I rode almost a mile & a half this morning to visit Albion & Capt. Hoyt - I found that poor Albion had met a soldiers death, that I should see him no more on Earth again - He was shot through the body on the 2d of June & died on the 3rd - Capt. Hoyt, who is in the Brigade Staff, expresses the greatest regret at the loss of Albion, he had the entire charge of Capt. H's Co. and was acknowledged to be the best orderly in the regiment, always prompt and faithful in the discharge of his duties and a brave and gallant soldier - He had been recommended for promotion, and if he

had lived would probably soon have obtained a Lieutenants Commission - He was one of the few, who though under so much of the evil influence of army life, did not fall into <u>one</u> bad habit of the army - On the other hand his Captain told me he was a <u>better</u> boy than when he left home - His life is an example of a Christian patriot that is truly noble - Not many have rendered such faithful service to their country as a soldier as he, not many Christians have been so devoted & true to God, as this noble boy has been. Under all the trying circumstances of his life as a soldier - It is sweet to know that he is now far from all the sounds of war & at peace with the Savior, whom he loved so well...

Union troops advancing on Confederate lines at Cold Harbor, Virginia.
Reverend Thompson's friend, Albion Brooks, was wounded at Cold Harbor
on June 2, 1864 and died the following day.

As with the fall of Fort Sumter, the unbelievable news of the disaster for the Union forces at Manassas prompted Reverend Thompson to write that when he found that a friend's "*soul was in bitterness over the terrible tidings from the war*", the Reverend still "*insisted that it must be exaggerated*". However, regardless of whether the reports were exaggerated, Thompson was up early the morning of July 23 to get a flagpole, because even if the news was "*at its worst there was no such time as this very moment for resolutely sending up the dear flag*". Outwardly, he tried to keep everyone's spirits high, but in the privacy of his diary, Thompson admits that there is "*grief every where at the war news*" and he felt it most deeply.

On July 24, there was still some confusion as to what actually occurred at Manassas and Thompson recorded the following in his diary:

The tidings are bad enough but for all every day, mails bring home reduction from the first statements. A fearful panic & flight cannot be doubted but it is not so bad as at first reported. There was no pursuit & that was singular if we were really beaten & the enemy knew it. The effect of the news is very depressing and yet Gods grace that good may come of it. Less confidence in ourselves and more in Him.

112

In the following days, Thompson's immediate concerns about the war were overshadowed by the illnesses of his children. The family's friend and doctor, Robert Hubbard, (who would enlist with the 17th CT in August, 1862) diagnosed "*inflammatory dysentery*", which was severe enough to cause Thompson and his wife to fear for the life of at least one of their children. Dysentery was more than just an unpleasant illness, it could be fatal, for children and for soldiers.

In October of 1862, a Sergeant Cooley wrote to Thompson complaining of the same illness and indicated that the source of the disease was most likely that age-old problem for army camps, the water.

I have been unwell for some time. I do not like the water. I think it is very bad for us. The biggest part of the Regiment lives with Bowel complaint. At the Surgeons tent there are about 75 to 100 men every morning sick. I have had the complaint for 6 weeks with hardly any cessation. I have a disease that with a little excitement causes the bowel complaint to come on.

Sergeant Cooley's solution to the problem?

I think I shall have to get a discharge from the Army. I can I think for I know that I am not a military subject. I guess that there will be a good many that will have to be discharged or there will be some soldiers graves mounds here.

Apparently, Sergeant Cooley had not been in the army very long and did not realize that discharges were not handed out to everyone who felt that they were not a "*military subject*". However, disease was a serious problem for both Union and Confederate troops, with over 60% of all deaths during the war being attributable to disease. That is a staggering percentage considering that the total number of casualties for the war was approximately 600,000.[58]

In addition to contaminated water, bad food and poor sanitation, a major killer was infection. Conditions at field hospitals, or any hospitals during the 1860's, were hardly aseptic and if a wounded soldier survived the surgery (frequently involving amputation), he was often later overcome by severe infections and gangrene. Given a choice, most soldiers during the Civil War would probably rather have faced an enemy with a gun, than the terrible unseen enemy of bacteria.

However, circumstances were not only unhealthy and crowded on the field; towns had to find housing for the swelling numbers of recruits waiting to be shipped out. On September 18, 1861, Thompson recorded that he "*was greatly pained to find in what a wretched shed miscalled 'barracks' our soldiers are put at Hartford & how pig-like they are left to scramble for their food*". Many men did not even have the luxury of barracks and had to contend with Mother Nature along with everything else.

---

[58] There were more casualties during the Civil War than Americans suffered during all its other wars combined, including WWI, WWII, Korea and Vietnam.

To Reverend Thompson from Franklin Hull, 9th Regiment Connecticut Volunteers, Camp Gayles, West Meriden , Connecticut, January 21, 1862:

We are still in camp waiting all in good health and spirits, but very badly quartered it hails, rains & snows almost every day. it seems as though Uncle Sam had forgotten us entirely but I guess its all right. we cannot drill on account of ice. we dare not cork our Horses, they cannot stand up and its rather rough for both man and horse. we pass the time writing & singing . our work principally is feeding ourselves & Horses & standing guard perhaps we may have more to do one of these fine days...10 good fellows crowded into a place [tent] with all our equipment in a space about 12 ft square. when we want to stretch or turn over we have to crawl out. we have a little stove - about the size of a tea Kettle, to warm us by, its better than nix...our Maj is strict Lyon is his name. the Artillery has gone their destination is for Royal I believe, they were mighty glad to get away from this icy Country, happy as clams in the mud. I tell you we wanted to go with them...Friend Thompson will you do me the favour to call on my family. I am troubled about them. my wife and boys are very dear to me and I Know it will be a comfort to them and a great Kindness to me...

Reverend Thompson was to work throughout the war to help to improve conditions for soldiers and their families, both materially and spiritually. The following letter from a soldier by the name of Ritchie (who had enlisted but didn't know it because he was drunk at the time) illustrates the fact that many soldiers could use all the help they could get.

Key West Barracks [Florida]
3rd October 1861

Rev AR Thompson
My dear Sir

I have not had the pleasure of hearing from you or of you for a long time, I having I may say been out of the world for a few months past - But before I give you any news about myself I must apologize for my rudeness and want of consideration in visiting you on two occasions at Bridgeport, where in a state of health which must have made it very embarrassing to you and Mrs. Thompson particularly - of course at the time my perception was not of the clearest kind, but I have since had plenty of opportunity of reflection upon my folly, exemplified in a thousand ways, and those visits to you had troubled me not a little. It would almost seem as if I were incorrigable and think my besetting sin had rivetted its chains upon me beyond any hope of relief. About the beginning of June while in a fit of Delerium I somehow or other got into (?) Zouaves Regiment NY Volunteers and knew nothing about it till two days before we sailed for Fort Pickens. I have suffered under the circumstance. I could have procured my discharge but on reflection I concluded to see the thing out hoping that it might have some salutory effect in the future if spared, and I thought it would be some slight atonement to society if I should lose my life in what I consider to be a just and honorable cause - The life is hard enough and like most others I wish we saw indications of a termination to the war, but so far I have not regretted joining the Army, although I must say I wish I had stumbled into any other Regiment. With a little more discipline they will make good soldiers...We had a miserable three successive months on Santa Rosa - We were outside the Fort in tents that were equally accommodating to the burning rays of the sun and the torrents of rain that alternated - The whole Island is white sand and sand was everywhere in your hair in your shirt your food and drink. Still the men on the main remained healthy and we had not a

U.S. Army tents on the white sands on Santa Rosa Island, Florida.

single death - allowing there were several among the regulars - On the 1st of September we were ordered to Tortugas (I mean Company A)...We have good barracks here and our rations are much improved, having fresh meat and Potatoes generally three times a week - Key West is under Martial Law and the Guard Duty is pretty heavy but there is little likelihood of our having any fighting here. We long expected it at Fort Pickens and I

Fort Pickens.

expect they will have it hot and heavy before long[59] - We have had no mail from the North here for some time and we expect duly to have important news from "Old Virginia". I hope you will write to me when you have leisure - and give me any news you may have heard - I have had no letter from Mrs. Ritchie since some time in March and I am anxious to hear of her and the children - It is a strange life I have been leading of late years and who knows how it will end, but I trust I have "(?) into the wilderness to learn wisdom" - I am happy to say that I have at present a perfect horror of drink, and I never (?) take it though it is plentiful here - I hail this as an encouraging symptom...I hope I shall be able to seek grace to assist me in overcoming this awful sin and curse...I was prosperous and had everything that hearts could wish. Few young men in business in New York were more generally known and respected than I - And I can trace to this habit the loss of means and business (?) , the loss of confidence, the loss of a comfortable

---

[59] Battles were fought at Fort Pickens on October 9, 1861 and March 27-31, 1862.

house and now I may say I am a penniless wanderer. Alas alas. But I will not despair or repine. I deserve more in this world than I have yet suffered...

Thompson was to console many such sufferers, and while numerous people wrote of the inspirational power of his words, words could be misconstrued and twisted, especially in times of war. Thompson appears to have gotten into a sticky situation when someone did misquote him, and the misquote was published in the local newspaper.

September 6, 1861 diary entry:

The Standard of last night published a 'Secesh' [60] *letter from some Bridgeport woman to a woman in Macon Geo., Govt. at Washington intercepted it & sent it to (?) & they publish. In it she quotes me as having said in the pulpit that God was on the Southern side. Mr. Barnum*[61] *called to suggest that it must be answered & wished me not to reply directly thru the paper but to preach on the national crisis Sabbath morning. At first I refused - finally after reflection I agreed.*

Thompson wrote to the *Standard* informing the paper that he would answer the accusation in church on Sunday. The response was overwhelming.

Sunday, September 8, 1861:

This morning preached the Sermon on the times which had been requested. Read Psalms 118:6 "The Lord is on my side. I will not fear what can man do unto me". The church was filled to capacity. Seats, aisles, galleries, spaces, pulpit, sofa & vestry rooms, they got the builders ladders from the church & put planks across them & stood on them outside the windows & with that hundreds went away who could not get in. The Lord helped me. I tried to speak plainly, earnestly & kindly.

The sermon must have had its desired effect on the huge audience as there was no further mention of any attempts to link Reverend Thompson with secession. Unfortunately, this would not be the end of the troubles for Thompson in Bridgeport. Certain powerful members of the church were still stirring discontent.

October 23, 1861 diary entry:

Had some chat with Hubbell today in which he let out that E. Hawley had taken him in hand emphatically for what he called his troublesomeness viz his fidelity to me, informing him deliberately of the intention of certain men to rule the South Church & that if he did not hereafter keep quiet he must look out for himself. What remains of exposure to detect the conspiracy & stamp Hawley as the chief of the clan...This is really what I have had to contend with under the sleek guise of gentleness. 'Having obtained help of God I shall continue to this day'. It is better to trust in the Lord than to put confidence in men.

---

[60] A term used to describe those who supported the South's secession from the Union.

[61] The famous showman, P.T. Barnum.

What little confidence Reverend Thompson had in his position in the South Church diminished to the point that, early in 1862, he decided to leave Bridgeport. While there may have been some who were against him, not everyone was happy to see Reverend Thompson leave them.

Whereas:

We, in common with the multitudes, in and around our City; have heard with heartfelt sorrow, that the <u>Rev. A.R.</u> <u>Thompson</u> is soon to leave the City of Bridgeport, and

Whereas:

We desire to manifest our esteem, and present to him Some Substantial token of our good will; therefore be it

Resolved:

That the Rev. A.R. Thompson during the three years he has dwelt among us has; by his Eloquence and bold condemnation of Sin, in the pulpit: by his Ministrations to the needy: and by his energy and public Spirit in our midst; contributed much to the personal good of the people; the welfare of our City, and endeared himself to our own hearts.

Resolved:

That we earnestly commend him for the tender Sympathy & Kindness he has ever shown toward his fellow man of whatever name or place; and Humbly trust, we may be led, through the influence of the Holy Spirit to profit by his teachings and Emulate his example.

Resolved:

That words cannot express the Sorrow we feel at his leaving us; but we trust and believe it is wisely ordered by our Heavenly Father, for a more extended Sphere of usefulness in this life; and for his eternal gain hereafter.

Resolved:

That we request the acceptance of Mr. & Mrs. Thompson from our hands; of accompanying presents as a Slight testimonial of our regard.

Reverend Thompson's "*Sphere of usefulness*" would indeed extend far and wide. In March, 1862, he was installed at the 21st Street Dutch Reformed Church in Manhattan, but more importantly, that month he also joined the New England Soldiers' Relief Association at 104 Broadway. He remained at the Relief Association for the rest of the war, preaching, tending to the sick and wounded and giving final words of comfort to the hundreds of men he was to see die there.

Rev. Mr. Thompson.

Rev. Mr. Thompson preached his farewell sermon at the South Church last evening.— The church was literally jammed, every seat being taken, aisles and lobbies filled, and many occupying the lecture room at the side, the windows between it and the church being opened so as to afford extra accommodation for the audience. The members of the City Guard were present, he having been Chaplain of the Company since its organization. In his sermon he sketched the progress of the church during the three years of his ministry, showing its rapid increase and the firm stability it now enjoyed.

Rev. Mr. Thompson during his residence here has made himself beloved by a large circle of friends and acquaintances, not merely in the congregation over which he has been Pastor, but among other denominations. As a preacher he was eloquent, fervent and sincere. The Christianity he expounded was of a practical kind, and to precept he added practice by deeds of charity to the suffering, advice and paternal counsel to the erring, and encouragement to those who were seeking to do right.

Ever since this rebellion has raged he has espoused the cause of the Union, has endeavored to rouse up dormant patriotism, and to urge that loyalty is not merely to be shown by words but by acts. He has taken a great interest in the temporal and spiritual welfare of our volunteers, and by his earnest efforts much has been done for their comfort.

We are sorry that circumstances are such that he will leave us, but wherever he may go he will be followed by the best wishes of many devoted and loving friends.

Notice of Reverend Thompson's departure from the South Church, which appeared in the *Bridgeport Evening Standard,* Monday, February 24, 1862.

News From the Field : 1862

To Reverend Thompson from H.T. Hanford, Fernandina Florida, March 13, 1862:

I well recollect when I met you last and when & where I bid you farewell. Since then I have been in many places and been an actor in many scenes. The Regiment with which I was connected were not permitted to go on this expedition or to bear a part of the honors of this bloodless victory. The General's orderly and myself are the sole representatives of Conn that were permitted to come. My position in the Commisary Department makes it necessary for me to go wherever the majority of the Brigade are ordered. We here see the dreadful effects of this war upon those that reside in the seceded States. Most of the citizens that are left here (about 300 in number) are entirely destitute of the necessities of life, and they have no money but Southern scrip therefore our Government must and do provide for them. The work of reformation has commenced and this city begins once more to have the appearance of civilization. All able bodied men of

Union troops occupying Fernandina, Florida.

either color are given work in the Qr Masters Department and the gentler sex can do the washing for the soldiers. Col Harland a Rebel Officer who was decoyed on board one of our Gun Boats (sailing under French colors) the first day we came here has been very kindly entertained by our much loved and respected Gen Wright and sent to day to his friends under a flag of truce. The Rebels are burning everything for miles away. All places of any account near here are deserted. Gen Wright is now occupying the House formerly owned and occupied by Mr. Yuler (late NY Senator) who has seceded the second time. Do not think that because I am away from home and friends and those I love, that I forget them. No my thoughts often wander back to the days that are past, and the many pleasant days that I have spent in listening to your voice. I have not forgotten what was then a great source of pride and pleasure to me, my Sunday School Class. I often think how many times I was saved from temptation. But those happy hours are past and many yet will be the days ere I shall be permitted to look again on such a scene. But I hope and trust if ever I am permitted to return to my native land & home to be better prepared for the heavy responsibility resting on each and every one of us...Please remember me to all that remains of my old class...

To Reverend Thompson from Alfred le Roe, Head Quarters, 102nd N.Y. Volunteers:

...Last night in a tent near us some three or four fine singers had met and were carrying the entire score of each tune. They had fine voices which rang out clearly on the night air. Soon there was quite a knot around listening & they kept it up till late. At 'taps' when lights must all be out all went to their quarters delighted. How much better than card playing.

We are here at present constructing a large strong fort. Every day the enemy are firing upon us & there are frequently sad casualties. Day before yesterday my regt had two killed & one wounded by a single shot. God though is with us & our meetings behind the breastworks continue in interest & power Souls are converted, sins forgiven. Gods grace can triumph anywhere...

To Reverend Thompson from Sergeant Henry Cooley, Harpers Ferry, West Virginia, October 12, 1862:

...I hope the time is not far distant when this rebellion will be crushed out and we be allowed to go to our quiet homes again, and enjoy the blessings we have had to leave behind...Thus far we have had only hard bread to eat - now we are hoping to have soft bread and fresh beef twice a week & think it a real luxury, it is so long that some of the men will greet the soft bread with delight, it being so long since we toasted any. We buy some of it here at 10cts per loaf, not very long at that. Our Regt has been rushed through a course of discipline we did not expect so soon. I think now that we shall make this our winter quarters. These heights are in a terrible cold place or at least our camp is situated in one of the coldest parts of these heights, being situated on the very top of the bluff. It

Harpers Ferry, West Virginia.

has been storming now for three days, and it is quite cold. I hope that if we go into winter quarters here that we shall be moved down upon the hillside where the wind cannot strike us when it blows so bitter cold. Our wounded are getting along nicely. One of our company has returned from the hospital, the rest of the wounded have gone to Washington, one of them had his finger axidently cut off since he went to the hospital...

Worse Than Paris

The Baltimore Riot of 1812 was compared to the mob violence of the terrible days of the French Revolution in the streets of Paris. However, the riots which took place in New York City in 1863 are almost beyond comparison. Some of the same citizens Reverend Thompson saw crowd Union Square to catch a glimpse of Major Anderson with the flag from Fort Sumter and line the streets to cheer the troops in April of 1861, became murderous rioters just two years later.

The city's enthusiasm for the war had waned considerably in the two bloody years since it began. Public opinion was further eroded by the passing of the Enrollment Act; an act calling for mandatory military service for men 20-45 years of age. As if this new draft law wasn't bad enough, an individual could avoid service if he could find someone to take his place, or if he could pay the sum of $300. This final clause infuriated the poor, in particular the Irish poor, who also viewed free blacks as competition for their low-paying jobs. Believing that black people were responsible for the war, immigrants were unwilling to risk their own lives in the fight against slavery.

The Enrollment Act came into effect on Saturday, July 11. On Monday, July 13, a crowd of predominantly Irish immigrants set fire to the draft headquarters. Soldiers, police and firefighters could do nothing as the crowd swelled in size and began a savage rampage throughout the city; blacks being the main target. Black citizens were dragged from their homes, beaten and murdered. An orphanage for black children was burned to the ground. For three days New York City was the scene of an unbridled orgy of crimes of every nature.

Rioters hanging a black man on Carmine Street.

Order was not restored until Thursday, July 16, when troops of the United States Army finally put an end to the mob's brutal violence. The toll of the riots: dozens of buildings burned, millions of dollars worth of damage and over 1000 men, women and children murdered.

Although Thompson had left Bridgeport for New York, he remained in contact with his friends in the Connecticut regiments. In August, he purchased a chapel tent for the men of the 17th CT and at the request of his friend and commanding officer of the 17th CT, Colonel Noble, also served as an acting chaplain.

From Colonel Noble, Baltimore, Maryland, September 6, 1862:

I want you with us a short time as the acting chaplain of the reg. - I sent you a pass to N.Y. Col Almy...

The pass allowed Reverend Thompson to travel to Baltimore where the 17th had thought they would be spending just a few days before continuing on to join General Franz Sigel and the Army of the Potomac. However, the city was in a panic over raids conducted by Confederate cavalry and the 17th was ordered to stay and aid the garrison at Fort Marshall on the harbor, east of Baltimore. Anxious to fight, the 17th CT nonetheless did not see action until May of 1863, where they would receive their baptism by fire at Chancellorsville, Virginia.

At the Union defeat at Chancellorsville, the 17th CT suffered 120 casualties; Colonel Noble being among those who were severely wounded. The total number of casualties for both sides was once again staggering; 11,000 for the North, 10,000 for the South. During the bloody battle, the 17th CT had been positioned on the right of the Union lines, where Confederate General Stonewall Jackson attacked while General Robert E. Lee assaulted the center. Despite being outnumbered, the Southern forces scored a victory, but at a great cost. On the first day of battle, Stonewall Jackson was accidentally shot by his own men, had his left arm amputated and died eight days later.[62]

The 17th Connecticut, who had fought so valiantly at Chancellorsville, almost didn't make it there, due to some fighting which went on within the regiment two months earlier. In March, 1863, Thompson received an odd letter from Colonel Noble, who was with his regiment near Brooks Station, Virginia. The letter indicates that despite being brave under fire, Colonel Noble may not have been an ideal commanding officer; resorting to arresting most of his staff to solve what he perceived to be problems of the most serious nature, but were most likely due to a lack of control, if not extreme paranoia.

The arrest was made of so many of my officers after secretly caucusing and meeting and appointing committies and resolving and doing lots of other military things at the instigation of Brady [Major Allen G. Brady] *- They got up a petition without my knowledge and without any request to me before the subject, stating in such unsoldierly language but all with the plausible pretension that it was important to be led into battle by one who was accustomed to drill and maneuver them, and could do so. - Had they come to me with such a request, it would have been granted - But that was not what they wanted...to play into what they thought my weak spot that I could not drill them, and asked that I might be made to do so, It has so happened that except for a short time in*

---

[62] When learning of the loss of Jackson's arm, General Lee remarked of his most valued officer, "He has lost his left arm, but I have lost my right arm."

Faces of the 17th Connecticut

Historical Collections, Bridgeport Library.

Colonel William Noble

Historical Collections, Bridgeport Library.

Major Allan Brady

Historical Collections, Bridgeport Library.

Dr. Robert Hubbard

Historical Collections, Bridgeport Library.

Captain William Hubbell

Chantilly I have never had an opportunity to drill them...When I could at Stafford Court House I was on the Court Martial of the Regiment duty, till our (?) at Belle Plain, there was no opportunity for drill...At Washington we were all at work - work - work - At Baltimore we had about 5 weeks drilling time. Only about two weeks of this time had our Battallion drilled in full Battallion. It was to drill - drill by 1/2 Battallion under Brady - 2 1/2 under Walter[63] - this was on a strife between them to see which could do the best - and to bring the Regiment up to a high standard - and they did come up like a Rocket and when we arrived at Chantilly they drilled splendidly - but my poor arm was too much infected to dare such activity - as was required to drill on my horse - and I shall drill them in no other way for that is the way I shall try to do in the field and the fight -

But as I said, they thought they got me there - and so went to work in that most unmilitary way of caucusing & meeting & campaigning - getting up papers for all the world as if they were in Conn at the meetings - a course which if indulged in - would demoralize our army, for if its officers can and do - do so - men can and will - and instead of being an army we would be a mob - town meeting and political gathering style, cutting around and campaigning for names to this and that thing and against this and that man - Why manage things in this style and old Joe Hooker[64] could not leave the Army for 24 hours. There are a great many everlasting great men in this world in their own opinion, and think they know about every thing. Like Brady. They think they can be commander because he can drill a Co or Reg. Every thing would be at heads and points under such rule, and all chaos & confusion more confounded - The moment I found them out, I put a very quick stopper on the whole proceeding and arrested the whole batch of Lieutenants but 5, and all the Captains but 2, and Major Brady into the bargain - put them in close arrest that is confined to their quarters and when asked for larger limits replied that I did not deem it consistent with the reasons of their arrest, to permit them larger liberty, and that as soon as I deemed it proper I would notify them thereof - so I kept them all shut up for the better part of a week. I then released all the Lieutenants here and one of the Captains. The other Captains and Brady I have preferred charges against and they will be Court Martialed.

(Col Noble means only those men arrested who signed the petition)[65]
...Now you know I am as gentle as a Lamb - to those who appreciate my friendship and good rule to aid them, and that I will do for them whatever in me lies - but I believe nobody can drive me - I fear not ever to do right, ever not to do wrong... But enough the whole of it is that they have got to learn that <u>I am Col of this Reg</u>. and that I shall never again consider but my own judgment, as to what I shall do. And the brotherhood system is broken up. And under that cracked shell they will find a steel clad Armor and rigid hand - This was just what was wanted to bring the whole business of the Reg up to a strict Military Standard - now they will have drill in the field - drill at home - drill and exact rules in all they do - I shall treat them kindly but firmly - They are no longer my

---

[63] Lieutenant Colonel Charles Walter was killed at Chancellorsville, May 2, 1863.

[64] General Joseph "Fighting Joe" Hooker, had replaced General Burnside as commander of the Army of the Potomac.

[65] In several instances, Colonel Noble refers to himself in the third person.

*brothers, but my officers...I am absolved by their own act and now I am by myself - It
will be all the better...I will see they do their duty as soldiers, and that they do their duty
to the soldiers - who are many of them in every way particular, better than they are -
...Now the result of all this business will be that I shall stand higher with every soldier
and officer in the Regiment about here and if they remain in this regiment every officer
will recognise their Colonel -----Ah how good I sleep - glorious - that I know I am well...*

This unusual situation was resolved without a Court Martial, for any parties
involved. News of the resolution was conveyed to Reverend Thompson by his friend and
former family doctor, Robert Hubbard, who had become Surgeon-in-Chief of the 2nd
Brigade, 1st Division, 11th Army Corps. On April 12, 1863, Hubbard wrote:

*...Col Noble has settled all his differences - released his officers from arrest, gone
earnestly to work & is doing well.*

Dr. Hubbard was to play an important role in Colonel Noble's life; in fact, he may
have saved it. At Chancellorsville, Noble's left arm was wounded by a minie ball and his
left knee was wounded by a shell fragment. The more threatening wound was in the arm
and as the main artery appeared severed, doctors prepared to amputate. However, Noble
insisted on seeing Dr. Hubbard (even though Noble had previously written some rather
disparaging remarks about the doctor) and Hubbard did manage to save the arm.
Noble required two months of recuperation in Washington. He might have stayed
in Washington even longer, but when news of an impending battle reached him, he tried
to return to his regiment as quickly as possible. He found his men on July 4, on the
battlefield of Gettysburg, the day after the battle had ended. The 17th Connecticut had
seen heavy action during the battle at Barlow's Knoll and Cemetery Hill, sustaining 198
casualties. Among the wounded was the allegedly infamous Major Brady, who's shoulder
was wounded by a shell fragment. The three-day battle[66] in that small Pennsylvania farm
town would see the heaviest casualties of any battle during the war; approximately 23,000
for the North and 25,000 for the South. While the Union victory at Gettysburg marked a
turning point in the war, there would still be two long years of fighting, and dying.
Reverend Thompson would continue to do whatever he could for the soldiers. He
may not have been able to directly add himself to the strength of the Union forces, but he
tried to make the soldiers he met stronger by his words. The following letter dated May
29, 1864 was from a soldier named Ellis R. Williams, who had just attended one of the
numerous services Reverend Thompson conducted at the New England Soldiers' Relief
Association in New York City.

*Your sermon this afternoon has had a terrible effect upon my conscience, like the lion
annoyed and provoked in his den, thoroughly aroused as to its future condition...Permit
me to ask ere I leave again for my regiment that you will pray especially for me once.
Perhaps the prayer will be answered, and how I do hope it will. In the meantime I will
not forget to pray myself. Soldier's life is so very uncertain, hence this request. Us*

---

[66] The Battle of Gettysburg was fought on July 1-3.

soldiers, though we are very bad men, think and talk a good deal concerning your good sermons. Often before I have heard our own boys say, after returning home from a furlough, that the best preacher that they ever heard was one Mr. Thompson of New York. I can now tell the boys the same thing. We are satisfied that you are a true Christian yourself, and whatever you preach comes direct from the heart. Rest assured, dear sir, that although the soldiers do not put in practice what is preached to them, they nevertheless have such a deep feeling of regard and respect towards you, so much so, that your name as a soldier's friend and benefactor is on the lips of everyone, almost, in the army.

I remain your Most unworthy friend
<u>*Ellis R. Williams*</u>
Please name me to no person in the world, unless I be dead on the field of carnage, then you may, but then only.

<u>News From the Field : 1863</u>

During a year which saw terrible battles at Chancellorsville, Gettysburg, Vicksburg and Chickamauga, not all letters from the field dealt with the war.

To Reverend Thompson from Dr. Robert Hubbard, Head Quarters of the 17th Connecticut Volunteers near Brooks Station, Virginia, April 12, 1863:

I was greatly disappointed at not being able when in New York to shake you again by the hand but Martial Law is rigid and I could not wait...My call at your house was like going home and I enjoyed every moment of my brief stay for I have long loved you all... The roads are quite dry again comparatively although tonight a delightful April Shower is beating tattoo on my tent roof. I send Nettie [Thompson's daughter] the first fruits (or rather <u>flowers</u>) of Floras Kingdom here as well as in New England, a specimen of the Epigea Repens or Trailing Arbutus. It is an evergreen creeper of great beauty and fragrance but has hitherto resisted all efforts to seduce it from its native woodland to the garden - like the aborigines it withers at the touch of civilization...may I trouble you to purchase me a little good smoking tobacco & enclose the Bill for I cannot get from the Sutlers anything of the Kind that is tolerable and I cannot go without smoking occassionally...I hoped in this to have seen you in Old Virginia but I suppose you are fully occupied. You will please remember that your invitation is a standing one to visit the 17th, your kindness to the men will always be gratefully appreciated. Thank the ladies again for their kindness to strangers although they are <u>not all angels</u>...

P.S. I omitted to mention that when we move on again it will be to victory as I presume you take that for granted.

(Two weeks after writing this letter, the 17th Connecticut moved on to defeat at Chancellorsville and had to wait for Gettysburg in July to taste victory.)

Gettysburg

On July 1, 1863, General Robert E. Lee and his Southern troops approached the small, Pennsylvania town of Gettysburg from the north. Union General George Meade's Northerners approached from the south. The battle began a few miles north of town when Union General John Buford's cavalry encountered an advance guard of the Army of Northern Virginia. As Buford fought to maintain his position, word spread rapidly, and both great armies began to converge. By the end of the first day, Confederate forces had pushed their way into the town. Union troops fell back to a defensive position on Culp's Hill and Cemetery Hill.

On the morning of July 2, Union troops numbered about 85,000, while Confederate strength stood near 70,000. The Union forces, many of whom had marched through the night to reach Gettysburg, were stretched along a fishhook-shaped line of hills from Culp's Hill south to Little Round Top, and General Lee ordered that these hills be taken. As the battle resumed, fierce fighting occurred in places with names as ominous as the Devil's Den and the Slaughter Pen, and as deceptively innocuous as the Wheat Field and Peach Orchard. As the second day drew to a close, it became clear that the Union line had held; due in part to the delayed action of the Confederate forces which didn't attack until afternoon, allowing the Union lines to strengthen, as well as to the tenacity of men like Union Colonel Joshua Lawrence Chamberlain and the men who defended Little Round Top.

General Robert E. Lee, still firmly convinced that his troops were invincible, ordered another attack on July 3, at the center of the Union line. The man chosen to lead the attack was General George Pickett. The plan called for an intense artillery barrage from Seminary Ridge, followed by 13,000 Confederate troops emerging from the woods along the ridge, marching across a large, open field, toward the Union center. The results of Pickett's Charge were nothing short of slaughter, as Union cannons and muskets opened upon the exposed Confederate forces, killing and wounding three-quarters of them.

Fully one-third of the approximately 150,000 troops engaged in the Battle of Gettysburg were killed, wounded or captured. While there were still almost two years of war to come, this battle arguably signaled the beginning of the end. The smaller Army of Northern Virginia could not fully rebound from the enormous losses sustained at Gettysburg, while the Union's Army of the Potomac was prepared to fight the bloody battle of attrition. Confederate forces never again attempted to attack in the north and Union forces began their steady push southward.

Today, the battlefields of Gettysburg National Military Park stand as a poignant reminder of the courage and sacrifice of both North and South. If there is truth to the words of Joshua Lawrence Chamberlain that in "*great deeds something abides*", then it truly abides in the silent fields of Gettysburg.

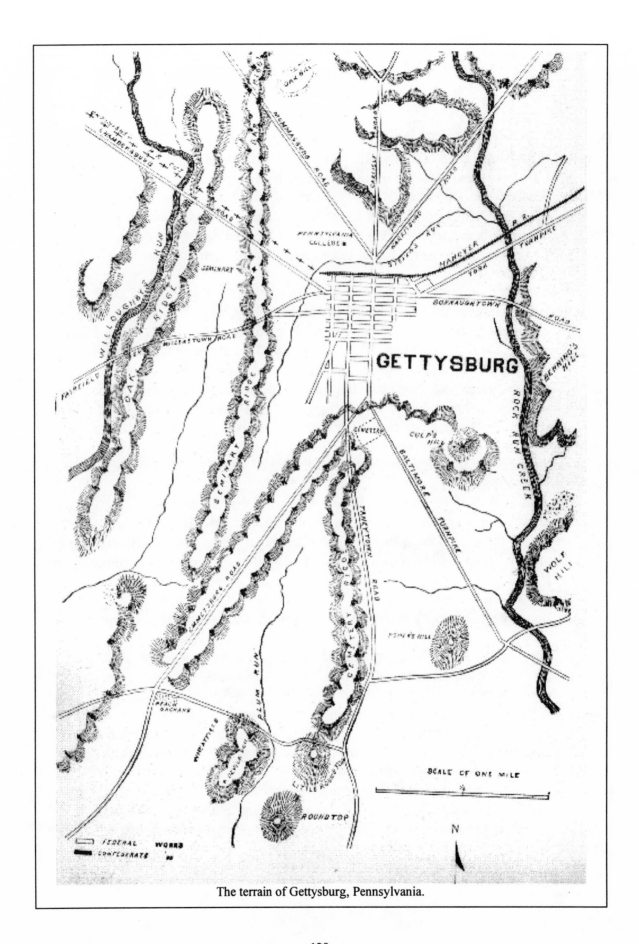

The terrain of Gettysburg, Pennsylvania.

Vanity and Vicksburg

From the middle of May until July 4, 1863, the Union's unrelenting siege and bombardment of the Confederate city of Vicksburg, Mississippi, left over 20,000 people dead, wounded and missing. The triumphant Union forces were led by General Ulysses S. Grant, who attacked the Confederate forces on land while Union Admiral Porter's gunboats bombarded the city from the river. The inhabitants of Vicksburg withstood horrific conditions; living in chambers dug into the ground and eating whatever they could find to survive. The city finally surrendered on July 4, knowing that they could receive better terms from the Union on the anniversary of American independence. The city of Vicksburg would not hold a Fourth of July celebration again for the next 81 years.

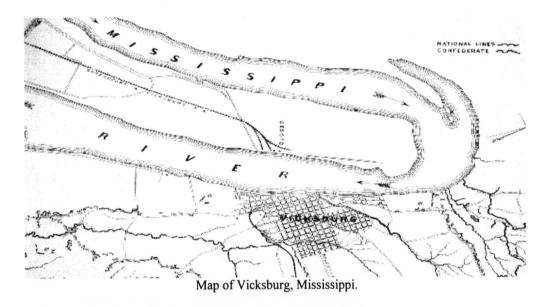

Map of Vicksburg, Mississippi.

The following letter to Reverend Thompson illustrates the fact that even at important moments in history, human nature is still human nature.

On board Transport Diana
Opposite Vicksburg July 2 [1863]

My dearest Pastor
Since I last wrote to you we have been tossed around considerably... Com. Davies fleet are just above Vicksburg they are showering in some of their shell into the batteries I can see their shell bursts but I cannot see their boats. We have seen all of the bombardment most every gun and mortar that has been fired. It is now quite an old story with us I can go to sleep with the mortars firing shaking the boat. Even now they are pouring in their shells and it shakes the boat so that I cannot write very well. The firing of guns this evening reminds me of the Fourth of July. I would like to be home tomorrow I would take dinner with you but I think it will be a very long while before I will be allowed that privilege and pleasure. The way the war is going on now it seems to

me as if it would last another year. I say "come on McDuff and cursed be he who first cries hold! Enough." We are still at work on the Cut-off, but I think it will be a failure.

The Union forces attempting to dig the bypass canal in front of Vicksburg.

The river falls as fast as they can dig and besides this I do not think it will be much loss to the city as the channel opposite is from Ninety to three hundred feet deep. There I have just dropped a large blot of ink but I cannot help it now as the mail leaves very soon and I will not have time to get another piece of paper. The Captain of the boat has just been around and gave orders all lights out. So I must bid you good night.

July 3rd

There has been very little firing during the day. Capt Brooks of the Gunboat Kenebec formerly of Bridgeport came aboard our boat today. We were very glad to see him and everybody from B. We have now been on our transports since the 18th of June. Tomorrow is the 4th I think it will be one of the Blueist ones I ever spent. - Now I am going to ask one of the greatest of favors from you. I want you to purchase me a Surgeon's sword and Belt. It is just the same as a Non Commissioned Sword only a great deal more expensive. I ashamed most to ask you but I see the other Sergeant-Majors come out in such <u>big</u> style that I thought I would procure a better Sword. Our Non Com Swords are regular toad stickers. I would prefer a sword with a bronzed Metallic Scabbard instead of a bright brass one. You can get me one with a guard on the handle or not just as it suits your taste. And I would like if you could just as well as not purchase me a middling size woven silk sash. The Sword and Belt will cost - 18 or 20 dollars I think if not more. Get me a belt with neat chains plated instead of straps which attach it to the Sword...Have my name engraved on it and if Mother is any way inquisitive do not let her know the price of it just give her the impression that it was presented to me... I think that the Sword Sash and belt will cost from 23 to 30 dollars it is very expensive I suppose Mother would say but never mind I like my new position very much but I will not be satisfied until I receive a commission...The Sergt. Major of the 30th Mass. came out the other day at Guard Mounting like a Pea Cock with white pants and big Sash...I want you to use your own taste about the Sword, Sash and Belt get me a neat Sash, Some of the Swords have no Guard which are very pretty and neat get one of a common length...

John [9th Regiment Connecticut Volunteers]

P.S. Do not send me a Surgeon's Sash that is a green one but send me a red one...

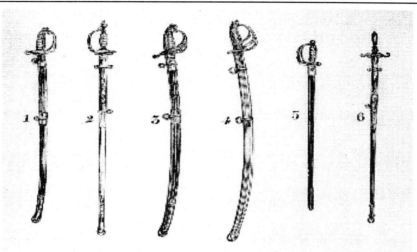

Swords of - 1. First Officer 2. General Officer 3. General Staff
4. Cavalry Saber 5. Musician & Noncommissioned Officers
6. Medical & Pay Departments

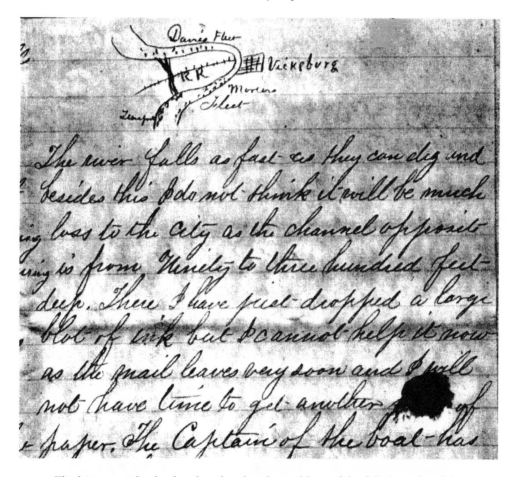

The letter contained a drawing showing the positions of the failed canal and the
Union fleet on the Mississippi River in front of Vicksburg. The spot of ink on
the page was the result of the boat shaking from the shelling.

News From the Field : 1864

To Reverend Thompson from Alfred le Roe, Chaplain of the 9th New York State Militia, Cedar Mountain, January 23, 1864:

Here I am now at my work. Work enough; in some aspects, discouraging enough. Open sin, profanity, drinking, to make your heart sick. Yet there are many men of intelligence in the ranks. Some of them have fallen, & would be sorely ashamed to have old friends know their present condition. Yet kind words & encouragement will help them to arise again. The reg was without a chaplain for fifteen or sixteen months...My Reg is the old N.Y. 9th State Militia, one of your city organizations. When they first came out, they were a very superior body of men. Only about 150 of their number remain. Nearly 200 have been commissioned as officers, Lieutenants, Captains, Colonels in other regiments. The 9th has recently filled up with the new three years men...

To Reverend Thompson from Captain William Hoyt, Head Quarters 3rd Brigade, 2nd Division, 2nd Army Corps, June 7, 1864:

Capt. Fiske , known in the literary world as "Dunn Browne", has died of wounds rec'd in the great battle in the wilderness, he was a settled minister in a church in Madison, Conn, much esteemed and loved by his congregation, he left his church not only, but a lovely wife & child and for two years fruitfully served his country as an officer in the 14th - On the resignation of our Chaplain last winter, Capt. Fiske was unanimously elected Chaplain of the regiment, he however declined, preferring to fight at the head of his Co, saying at the same time, that until a Chaplain was obtained he would perform any of a Chaplains duties...He was greatly beloved by all who knew him - The last time I saw him he was lying pale & feeble on a blanket at the Division Hospital, yet cheerful & resigned to God's will, ready as a Christian to meet death which seemed so probable - only a few hours before I had noticed him in the fierce battle in the wilderness, amid the roar of that awful fight in the woods, encouraging on his men - now he is dead - Twelve officers in our regiment have been killed and wounded in this campaign, over 80 officers in our Brigade, we have lost 1300 men - among them some of the best & bravest - Thirty five days we have marched and fought, only two days out of the thirty five have passed without fighting - You can not imagine what the Army of the Potomac has suffered & endured, I have seen men so exhausted with fatigue & work, as to get asleep while marching along this road, & not only this, but on picket within pistol shot of the enemy, I have seen <u>two thirds</u> of the whole picket line <u>asleep</u> in this most important duty, and though the penalty was death and the men knew so much depended on their watchfulness, yet they <u>could not</u> keep awake, and I hadn't the heart to have them punished - Too much cannot be said in praise of our brave soldiers. I have seen our Brigade charge through a fierce fire (a belt of burning forest) through tangled underbrush & over an abatis [an obstacle of sharpened sticks] , *to rebel earthworks,*

A Court Martial at Washington, has sentenced about 30 soldiers to death for various offences. It is probable that the lives of some of these men will be spared, but others will certainly be executed. A prisoner named Scott, of a Vermont Regiment, found guilty of sleeping on his post, will be shot, to-day — the sentence having been confirmed by Gen. McClellan.

A news item in the *Bridgeport Evening Standard*, September 9, 1861.

through a storm of bullets that seemed almost certain death to face - this was done on the 10th of May...I have seen the same brigade, unmoved by thousands of panic stricken men running in the rear, advance double quick to the charge and repel Longstreet's grand assault, which as nearly proved successful on the second day of the wilderness - Our brigade is better known as Carroll's Brigade (3rd Brig 2d Div.) - Carroll was wounded through the arm in the first day's fight but would not leave the field till he had his other arm broken by a bullet the day after the glorious charge of the 12th of May - I am proud to belong to this brigade of which I have spoken & to Hancock's 2d Corps.

God has been very merciful to me thus far, through all my perils I have escaped uninjured, in my duties as a Staff Officer of the Brigade I have had two horses shot under me, my blankets pierced with a bullet, my haversack shot through and a fragment of an exploding shell has slightly bruised my leg - I am happy to say that my friend Will Hinks is still unhurt though he has been hit with several spent bullets & one passed through his hat - We are now within 10 miles of Richmond and the siege of the rebel capital has commenced, the final result I doubt not will be our complete success, we have great faith in Grant and in our brave army. The rebs have fought admirably but do not I think fight now with the spirit they did at first, they are growing dismayed -

In case I am killed in this campaign and my body is sent home will you please be kind enough Mr. Thompson to assist in the funeral ceremonies.

To Reverend Thompson from Hiram Manville, 2nd Connecticut Light Battery, New Orleans, Louisiana, November 1, 1864:

...while I have been far from home and kindred and amid the din of war and the strife of Battle and through all the changing scenes which I have passed by land and by sea as well as on the tented field I have not forgotten the blessed truths and instructions which I have heard from your lips...I think I can truly say that I have experienced more happiness while I have been in the army than I ever did before in all my life...

133

Throughout the four tumultuous years of the war, Reverend Thompson's comforting and inspirational words reached more eyes and ears than he could have imagined, both in the United States and abroad. In January, 1865, an English boy, Matthew Agar, who had come to America earlier in the war to fight for the Union, died at the New England Soldiers' Relief Association. While Thompson had the unfortunate task of writing hundreds of letters to families who had lost loved ones, he took the time to compose sensitive and compassionate letters. The following excerpts from the 20-page letter he sent to Agar's parents illustrates this fact, and it was so touching that the family printed thousands of copies which were distributed throughout England.

From Reverend Thompson to Mr. Agar, Springfield House, York, England:

New York Jany 26, 1865

My dear Sir

> *I am a stranger to you. But God has called me in His providence to fulfill to you one of the most painful duties to which I ever have been summoned. I am the chaplain of the New England Soldiers' Relief Association in the city of N.Y.*

> *My duties there have brought me in connection with your Son Matthew Agar of the 8th Regt. New Hampshire Vols.*

> *Your Son has often spoken to me of yourself and his Mother as being true and devoted christians. Let me entreat you then, my dear Sir, to ask God for grace to enable you to receive the sad news which I am compelled to announce to you. Your dear Son has received his discharge from all earthly toil and service. God has been pleased to take him to himself in heaven.*

> *I have no words to tell you how dear & beloved Matthew became to us all. He won our respect & esteem & love. I do not feel as a stranger to you - Your dear boy spoke of you & his Mother so often - so reverently - so tenderly that altho' an ocean rolls between us I feel that you are no strangers to me. Your sorrow is my sorrow. Your beloved became my beloved. And the bitter cup which I am compelled to present to your lips, to-day was presented first to my own. I do not know how I can better fulfill my sad task to you than by giving the simple recital just as it happened of our sweet & pleasant intercourse with him until the angels of God took him out of our hands to heaven. For, my dear Sir, Your son died a humble, devoted christian. If I live to next Easter Sunday morning I will have completed the 20th year of ministry, In that time I have stood by nearly 700 dying beds, and I have never in them all seen calmer, clearer, sweeter, more intelligent & self possessed & yet more humbly trustful peace & repose on the blessed Saviour of Sinners than God enabled your Son to manifest...*

> *He came to us from the Department of the South late in November along with a number of soldiers weak & feeble, like himself. Making my round as usual among the cots on which lay the new comers I came to him - I sat down by his side and after saluting him according to my habit, said to him, - When did you come in? he told me that he was of the squad just in by Seas from New Orleans. I inquired then about his sickness and he told me, that like the rest of them, he was suffering from chronic Diarrhea, complicated with fever and ague. At that I congratulated him that he was having a furlough & supposing*

him to be a native born and on his way home, I said, - "Well you will have the right kind of medicine now for I have noticed that nothing brings one up who is troubled with this malady like home nursing.

Then he turned his face to me & said with inexpressible sadness, "I have no doubt of it sir but my home is on the other side of the sea."

His answer cut my heart like a knife, but I instantly replied - well you are the very fellow we want here then and we are the very people for you -"We will try to be Mother and father & sister & brother to you, - and if you want for anything that we can give you body or soul it will be your own fault for not asking for it." Then two silent tears ran down his face till they wet his pillow...

His symptoms for a while were favorable. In my Diary under date Decem. 19, I find the entry, - We get quite cheerful about Matthew Agar, - His symptoms mend decidedly, - but then they slip back again so rapidly that we almost lose heart & hope. I think there is no doubt that God is revealing himself to him in Christ & taking his hope upon the rock, ever blessed be his holy name / So it was with varying development in the main cheerful, until after Christmas and then his bowels began to ulcerate, and he began to lose ground rapidly. - Literally as his outward man perished his inward man was renewed day by day. Before this he had been able to walk or be carried to the rear wards of the hospital floor where, laid on a lounge, by the side of the rail enclosure, (a large open space of 12 or 15 feet square that runs up thru the whole building for ventilation) he could hear and join in on religious services held in the room below. I always stood where he could see me from the floor above & could notice him following fervently in the service. The last week of the year he became so feeble that he could no longer leave his bed...

God seemed to give him the peace that passeth all understanding & he never lost it again to his dying moment. From that time it was like being on the verge of Heaven to be near him. He knew he was failing but had a firm clear grasp of Heaven. I have the entry in my Diary under Jan 3rd - 1865 Matthew begins to fail physically with great rapidity. I dread lest the service of yesterday's twilight should be too much for his feeble sinews. But it was not. There came no reaction. He seemed to go up into Heavenly calm before our eyes...

Under Jan 4 my diary says...The Surgeon has abandoned all hope of his recovery. Nothing can be done now but to make him comfortable - poor boy away from home & Mother & sister & the chosen of his heart...

As he himself saw that his end was near he gave us your name & address and laid the solemn charge on us that we should write to you as we are doing. "Be careful, Chaplain" said he "to tell my mother that I died a christian in the faith of Jesus Christ, and in the hope of the hope of the resurrection, give her my dear love and also write to Miss Annie Gregory said he, and tell her I was faithful and true to her to my dying breath and I trust we shall meet in heaven."...

The day before he died he distributed some little gifts & tokens among his fellow soldiers who had been uniformly been exceedingly kind to him, lifting him as tenderly as they would an infant, after he had done that he sent out and bought a Bushel of Oranges, called up all the maimed & crippled soldiers to his bed and filled their hands with Oranges and then sent one to every sick man's cot in the hospital ward. The entry in my

Diary Jan 6 gives the last precious memorial of him thus - Hurried this morning to the Hospital. Matthew had been somewhat restless. He greeted me lovingly. I knelt and prayed with him -Then at his request I took the Bible and read to him...Then he dropped into a doze - presently he awoke & grew restless, could not get in an easy position - we changed his pillows, cushioned his knees up, & tried every way to relieve him, - I said Matthew dear the hour has come - this is beyond our reach. We would help you if we could. But dying is dying...Last night when Mrs. Russell the matron had made him comfortable for the night, as she smoothed his hair back from his forehead & kissed him He thanked her and said "Kiss me again for my mother," & she did so & then he said, "Kiss me once more for the girl I love," & she did. He failed now rapidly...I took his hand in mine, knelt down by his side commending his parting spirit to his father God. When I ceased praying there was just a quiver of life about his lips and in a moment that was over. It was just 37 minutes past 12 o'C Jany 6. 1865. He died so calmly and peacefully that we stood silently around his bed for several minutes expecting to see his lips quiver again, but it did not. Then I closed his eyes with my own hand, and Mrs. Russell cut a lock of hair from his dear forehead for his Mother...

He was laid in a neat coffin of Rosewood & over it was laid the flag for which he devoted his dear life - on his bosom we laid fresh flowers ... His precious dust was borne to the "Cemetery of the Evergreens" on Long Island about 5 miles out in the suburbs of this city where it reposes among that of his brother soldiers until the resurrection of the just...

Your son became as dear to <u>me as my own brother</u> ...

In August, Mrs. Agar wrote to Mrs. Russell, informing her that the "*inestimable letter of Mr. Thompson*" which was "*much prized*", was sought after by many people in England. In fact, the letter was in such demand that "*thousands of copies of it were printed in Sheffield*", to be distributed throughout the country. Mrs. Agar also related some details about Matthew's life, in particular, that he had been "*led astray by gay associates and lost his excellent situation*" in London. As a result, Matthew had decided to go to New York to find employment and his parents had not been aware that he had joined the Union Army until shortly before his death.

At Mrs. Agar's request, Mrs. Russell and Mr. Thompson had sent photographs of themselves, which Mrs. Agar intended to have "*framed and hung one on either side of my beloved Boy's likeness over the Mantle piece*". She also sent a picture of her son to Reverend Thompson, who kept it the rest of his life.

The Innocent Suffer

The following letter from Mrs. M. Mitchell to Reverend Thompson at the New England Soldiers' Relief Association, dated November 17, 1864, is one of the most compelling in the Ricca Collection. It is a poignant, first-hand account of how the Civil War devastated the lives of men, women and children.

Dear Sir

You are aware that I have been for the last few days been sharing the kind hospitality of Mrs. Russell. I was a listener at your Meeting last night and I assure you although I have nothing but unfaithfulness to mourn over in my spiritual life yet I felt like saying tis good to be here. I once enjoyed the comfort of Religion but I was away from church and my duties neglected I lost that enjoyment that I once had...After I was married...Everything seemed to prosper - I would tire you to give you a full History of all, but we lived on the Penninsula near the James River 2 1/2 miles from Petersburgh we had a Fine place 140 acres of Land well stocked we had everything hearts could wish for enough to spare I can truly say no poor ever came to the place but went away well suplied, for more than 2 years after the war commenced we lived in <u>fear</u> but unmolested, the Rebels came every day for something My Husband could not bear the Idea of feeding them but I know we were in there power and it was best to get along peacably but after all our kindness to them My Husband was taken Prisoner by Stewart of the Black Horse Cavalry he had been sick before leaving home I advised him not to go but he went and in five weeks he died from <u>Hemerage of the Lungs</u> that was a great trial, but a few weeks after Stewart sent a Requisition for us to leave the place I did not notice it imediately Till Mosby's Gerillas came I had no alternative, but some of the oficers of the Rebels advised me to go to Richmond to head quarters I did not go till they came and forced me, now I was <u>without Home</u> or <u>Friends</u>, after many hard ships I got up on the Road near Culpeper I knew a Family whom I had helped a good deal, who had a year before lived in Petersburgh, I went to them and all I had was what I had on and a good watch & chain, I commenced very humble I assure you I <u>Baked Pies and Cakes</u> and done very well in my humble way. Thought soon to have enough to come <u>north</u> to go into some kind of Business, where I could support myself and children who my <u>sister</u> has I had sent them to school previous to the war, but again the Rebels put some obstruction in the R. Road, killed 15 and about two thousand soldiers were sent from Wash. to Burn destroy everything on the Road so the Inocent had to suffer for the Guilty, I had not any warning I was not thinking of such a thing hapening Oh! My dear Friend what to do and where to Fly to I knew not, I felt many times like giving up in <u>despair what I have suffered never will be known</u> I have often asked myself what have I done that I should be so afflicted...I little cared wether I got anything to eat or not & felt as if there was no Humanity left for me I know I had always done all in my power for those in distress now I canot find employment when I am willing to work at anything. Oh! When I crossed the river in the Ferry how I did wish something might hapen that I would be drown. All the thoughts of my loving Husband Brothers My <u>House</u> being suspended from my dear children and knowing I brought not this trouble on myself then to be treated so cold by the world (that I used to think so good and full of charity) <u>you can scarce blame me</u> I felt as if God had forsaken me till I came only to get my Breakfast , as I had fasted a long time but Mrs. Russell, Oh her name will I hope be heralded all over the world for her <u>true good heartedness</u> but I must be brief she like the good Samaritan spoke to me so kindly and *not only spoke but acted and if I rise again which I hope I will she certainly has been the Instrument in the hands of God of at least making me feel as if I had something to live for Dear Pastor I do hope I can get Employment I understand housekeeping and am willing to work at anything. I would be thankful if you hear of something for me to do...I hope I will have the privilege of often hearing you speak for I shall long remember <u>last nights little Prayer meeting</u>. If you can in any way advise me I shall ever be gratefull*

> *Your humble Servant*
> *M. Mitchell*

Another soldier who was helped by Thompson at the Relief Association was Carl Koehler of the 25th Regiment of Massachusetts Volunteers. In February, 1865, Thompson received a letter in which the German-born soldier apologized for not writing sooner but as he "*never wrote letters in english*" before, he had been hesitant to write his first to a learned "*Reverend Gentleman*". Apologies completed, Koehler went on to compose an eloquent letter, writing, "*you will perhaps not so easily recollect me while you meet with so many soldiers together wich day after day and week after week do come and disappear like the waves on the ocean, but I recollect you and your words as fresh as if I was yet with you.*"

Koehler also wrote of his faith in God and informed Thompson that he was "*now three and a half* [years] *engaged in the battles of this country to help secure a substantial peace and liberty for ourselves who have enjoyed the blessings of freedom so far, and also for those who have been long in bondage, but besides this I strive to fight the battles of the lord to secure the peace of the soul...*"

Peace and liberty would finally come to the country when the war ended in the spring of 1865. On April 9, General Robert E. Lee surrendered to General Ulysses S. Grant at Appomattox Court House, Virginia.[67] However, it took time for news to spread to the South and the last soldiers of the army of the Confederate States of America did not surrender until May 26, 1865. However, news of another kind spread like wildfire across the nation.

On April 14, only five days after receiving the news he had longed to hear, President Abraham Lincoln was shot at Ford's Theater in Washington, D.C., and died the following day. Lincoln's assassin was the actor John Wilkes Booth. Although Booth wasn't aware of the terrible ramifications of his actions, when he pulled that trigger, he also killed the South's chances of a fair, and even compassionate, reintegration with the North, as Lincoln's successors were not so forgiving. On April 26, Federal troops trapped Booth in a barn in Bowling Green, Virginia, where he was shot and killed.

Justice for Booth's accomplices would quickly follow. On July 7, Mary Surratt, Lewis Powell, David Herrold and George Atzerodt were hanged for their parts in the plot. Several other conspirators were sent to prison at Fort Jefferson in the Florida Keys, otherwise known as the Tortugas.

---

[67] In an interesting twist of fate, the surrender occurred at the home of Wilmer McLean, who had lived near the first Battle of Bull Run. His home had been used by the Confederates as a headquarters during the battle. He had moved to Appomattox in the belief that he was removing his family from the intrusions of the war.

In September, an acquaintance of Reverend Thompson on board the steamer *United States* in the Tortugas wrote, informing him that "*Mr. Foster (a perfect gentleman) has sung this song several times & I asked him to write it off for me to send to you. I think it is one of the best (?) of the kind...written by Mrs. Howe of Boston...I am sure you will like it - I feel after hearing it sung like one inspired for the mark - I do think it is near Gods mark...*"

This inspiring song was the famous "*Battle Hymn of the Republic*", written four years earlier by Julia Ward Howe. Mr. Charles Foster did write down the words to send to Thompson and on the bottom of the sheet, added:

Copied on Steamship United States off "Tortuga" where
are confined the assassins of the Redeemer of his country.
September 27th 1865

Charles Foster

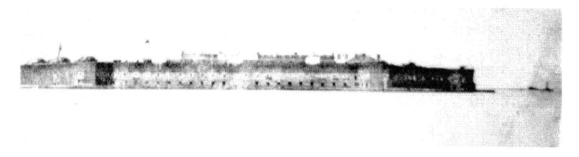

Fort Jefferson, where the "*assassins of the Redeemer of his country*" were held.

As the nation struggled to regain its footing after the tremendous devastation of the war, Reverend Thompson also tried to get his life back in order. On December 14, 1865, Reverend Thompson was conferred "*the Degree of Doctor of Divinity*" by Isaac Ferris[68], Chancellor of the University of the City of New York. Doctor Thompson continued in his duties at the 21st Street Dutch Reformed Church, but in May, 1866, went to Norfolk, Virginia. Whether the trip was official church business or a vacation isn't known, but in a letter to his daughter, Maggie, Thompson gives an account of the events in Norfolk during the war and a vivid picture of the sad condition of the post-war South.

I wrote to Pony[69] this morning & to Mother. In Pony's letter I gave him an account of our voyage down here - Your turn comes next. I am going to tell you something of this queer old town Norfolk... Norfolk is a queer, dull, old fashioned, terrible down looking place. I have not seen one handsome building in it except perhaps the church we were in last night & that was better looking inside than out. It is a very old

---

[68] Isaac Ferris conducted the funeral services at West point for Thompson's uncle, Lt. Col. Thompson in 1838.
[69] One day Thompson's son Alexander was becoming ill and complained that he "was a little hoarse". From that day Thompson called his son Pony.

place. There is one brick church[70] here which was built 40 years before the Revolutionary War. The rebels held Norfolk when our war began & kept it for quite a while. Long enough to diminish & destroy pretty nearly all its trade. Then one fine day, when they thought they had it all sure, with 10 or 12 forts all along the river as you come to it to knock anything to pieces that should come against it, one fine day what should old General Wool[71] do but cross over from Fortress Monroe with a good army away ever so far behind Norfolk where they hardly suspected that he could come. But he did, & marched up behind it & when the rebs found that he was coming they skedaddled out of Norfolk quick & Uncle Sam has held it ever since. When the war began for fear that the Union troops might come this back way & take Norfolk the rebs built a line of fortifications a mile long from one little river to another, & then they thought they had blocked it up all the way - We stood in the line of fortifications today - Like all the rest of the fortifications made for this war it is built by driving posts into the ground & then heaping sand over them. I broke off a chip from one of the posts which I will bring home with me. But when Gen Wool did come they only fired a few guns and hurried off - There is not anything much I can see about Norfolk accept colored folks. But such a town of darkeys I never did see before - Of all shades & sizes & especially little nigs. They swarm over the pavement like flies in a sugar barrel. I don't believe you ever saw so many of them together in your life as there are here. I really think that for every white person we have seen today we have seen 20 colored at least. The most of the white people here feel bitter & angry to think that the Union forces have succeeded & that colored people are free. Some are so angry that they can't hold them as slaves any more that they won't employ them to work on their farms & as they can't get any body else to work for them they just let their farms go to waste, which you see is biting their own noses off & very short too. Others are more sensible. But there is a good deal of angry feeling. But aren't the colored people glad to be free. Some are lazy & won't work & are bad. But a great many work a great deal better for being paid for it than when they were slaves. All through the nearly 30 miles that we have been riding today there are little patches of land in the woods, in the swamps even, where some black man who used to be a slave but is free now, has cut down the trees, & burnt out the bushes, & built a little cabin of logs or board & is now ploughing or sowing. OH what a poor country this is. Not the soil, that is good enough. But the people seem to have managed it so badly. For long long reaches all the fences are gone & all the bridges over the little streams are a few rails laid down. And the roads are horrible. The houses are mostly very poor & mean - Built with chimneys outside of them thus this queer shape. We haven't seen a decent cow today, and only two or three at that. The cattle were all killed off in the war for the soldiers to eat. Very few horses. They were all taken for the rebel cavalry - Mostly mules are used - And the most of them have the letter U.S. branded on their hips behind showing that they have been bought from the United States...We had a great deal of talk with our colored driver who used to be a slave & was very sensible. I shall have a good deal to tell you about when I get home please God more than I can write...

---

[70] St. Paul's Episcopal Church was built in 1739 and was the only building in Norfolk to survive when colonists burned the city in 1776 to keep it from the British.

[71] General John Wool was a veteran of the Mexican War and in his late seventies during the Civil War.

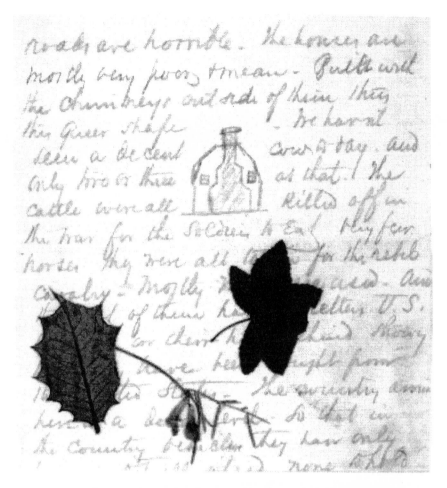

Reverend Thompson's letter to his daughter in which he sketched a house
in Norfolk. He also enclosed leaves and flowers from the countryside.

Throughout Thompson's travels, he wrote detailed letters such as this one to the
many members of his family and they, in turn, wrote frequently to their "*dear Papa*". In
all these pieces of correspondence, it is evident that there was deep and genuine affection
between Thompson, his wife and their children, even after the children had grown and
had families of their own. However, as much as Thompson loved his home and family, he
also obviously loved his travels, although they were far more than sightseeing adventures
as the following letter illustrates.

San Francisco Sept 23rd 1871

Dr Thompson
      Dear Sir

    *It is with pleasure that I now take up my pen to write to you. And to try to thank
you, for the many kind things you have done, to our race In bringing us out of the
darkness, into light, and for your help in teaching us the way to Eternal life. It is a great
joy to me, and, I am sure to all the Christian Chinamen all over the world to know that by
following God, here in this world, we shall see the glories of the next...Oh how I wish that*

141

more of my Countrymen would embrace the Christian faith...I now wish to thank you in behalf of our little society, Chinese Young Men Christians Society, for the many kindnesses you have shown towards them in teaching them how to sing the praises of our Lord and also for the valuable presents you have presented to them, and for the interest you have taken in their wellfare. I am happy to say, that our Society is increasing in size, as also our Library...I am your friend and pupil

Gin Bon, Secretary Chinese Young Mens Christian Society

Photograph signed by Gin Bon.

Possibly the house in which Reverend Thompson lived while he was the chaplain for Roosevelt Hospital.

142

Shortly after returning from California, Reverend Thompson became chaplain of the newly-opened Roosevelt Hospital in New York City, at the request of the founder. As his obituary explains, his years at the hospital were "*the last great work of his life*". The following description is reminiscent of his work at the Soldiers' Relief Association during the war.

Nearly two hundred beds in the hospital are constantly occupied by sick and wounded folk. They come and go, and during the course of a year about 8,000 patients spend from a few days to months under its roof. The majority of these are utterly prostrate. For three days of each week for more than a score of years the chaplain has gone from bed to bed encouraging and comforting the sufferers. His broad experience in life and consecrated nature brought him into instant touch with the patients. He called each one by name, and moved the sympathetic chord of all...Thus he ministered. Men especially loved to have him come to them. Many have said to me, "He understands men." He supplied them with books and papers; and often from his very limited means gave them funds on leaving the hospital to meet their necessities...Many a useful life to-day dates its reformation to Dr. Thompson's wise and patient revelation of the power and love of God...Every Sunday afternoon he conducted a service in a large alcove that faces the men's accident ward. On the benches before him would gather from twenty to forty helpless and lonely men and women. His order of worship was that of our Church. It was set forth in a little book that also contained a hundred and fifty hymns, most of them written by himself. I have been told by discriminating judges, that they regarded Dr. Thompson as one of the most eloquent men of the age. Once a month he has preached for me, and always with rare power. But I venture to say that his hospital sermons excelled all his pulpit ministrations in the simple majesty of Divine message, in sympathetic helpfulness, and in appeals to the heart. Face to face with real suffering and need...He lost himself in his message, and so found himself...

Ministering to the sick and wounded did indeed appear to be how Thompson "*found himself*". He never seemed to find anything but disappointment in the churches like those in Bridgeport and New York City and was, by far, more suited to comforting the sick than catering to fickle and demanding congregations. Hopefully, all this experience with death and suffering helped ease his own personal pain in the last several years of his life, as "*blow after blow fell upon him. His wife, whose presence seemed absolutely essential to his peace and comfort, was, after a long and bitter illness, taken; brothers, sisters, and lifelong friends quickly passed away; and he stood all alone.*"

While he may have lost many of his friends and family, he was far from being alone. He still had his children and grandchildren, and he still had the veterans of the 17th Connecticut Regiment of Volunteers. On October 22, 1889, Thompson delivered the oration at the dedication of a monument to the 17th CT on Cemetery Hill in Gettysburg. The excursion to Gettysburg began at seven in the morning of October 21, at the train station in New Haven, Connecticut. A booklet printed later that year describing the event, lists all of the 211 participants, including General Noble, Hoyt, Hubbell, Middlebrook and other acquaintances from his Bridgeport days, as well as members from the 27th

Regiment of Connecticut Volunteers. Many family members of the veterans also attended; the booklet mentions that Reverend Thompson was accompanied by one of his sons, although the name was not given.

Despite the long, twelve-hour journey, the chronicler relates that "*it would be difficult to find a jollier two hundred*". Upon arriving in Gettysburg, they found that there "*seemed to be more hack drivers and boarding house runners than there were veterans*". The party was "*ordered by Colonel Blakeman to 'fall in rapidly,' and soon marched to the McClellan House, which had been assigned as the headquarters of the two regiments*", although a number of the veterans stayed at the Eagle Hotel.

After supper many of the vets strolled about the town to see if they could find any familiar traces of '63. The town is said to have increased about one-third since the war, but among the business streets, we could see but little change from what it bore twenty-five years ago. The majority of the houses are of brick, as are also many of the sidewalks. The present population of the town is about 4,000...Corporal George Hale visited the house in which he was held as a prisoner after the first day's fight...Bailey, of the Danbury News, was there and he says the roadways are paved with cobble stones, and from their appearance he should judge the street commissioner was killed during the battle of '63...

At 9:30, Tuesday morning, the Seventeenth regiment, headed by the Gettysburg G.A.R. band, and escorted by their comrades of the Twenty-seventh, marched to their monument, which stands on the lane skirting the foot of East Cemetery Hill...The location of the Seventeenth Monument is on the identical spot where our own Captain Burr captured the Louisiana "Tiger" color bearer.

After the monument was unveiled, Reverend Thompson delivered a moving oration, in which he undoubtedly used the full, magnetic power of his voice.

General Noble, Veterans of the 17th and 27th Regiments, and Friends:
The dews and rains of heaven for more than a quarter of a century have been obliterating the traces of the stupendous conflict that once swept over this broad valley. In the peaceful quiet in which it lies this autumnal day, but for its memorial stones, no stranger could suspect that once, its bosom had been furrowed by terrific war. There are but slender signs to show that its grain fields were ever trampled by the feet of contending hosts, and its green sward reddened by the life-blood of brave and heroic men...

There are no words at our command wherewith to describe the events which are inseparably linked in human memory, with the place wherein we are assembled; it is a relief to know that it is not incumbent on us to attempt their description...Our coming hither to-day is to do honor to the brave men, living and dead, who bore their faithful part in the awful crisis, and so far to allow the memories of it, at once tremendous and tender, to sweep over us, as to render to them the honor which is their due...

Thompson continued by comparing Gettysburg with the great battles throughout human history. He also described with remarkable insight how the quest for freedom had

Thompson family.
Reverend Thompson as he may have looked at the
time of the dedication of the monument at Gettysburg.

evolved over the centuries and first found expression in the Revolutionary War. After congratulating the "*Men of Connecticut*" for their state's part in the nation's several struggles for freedom, he concluded:

Veteran soldiers of the 17th Regiment; brave, true, faithful men, this memorial stone, unveiled by the gentle hand of the fair child of one of your number, will remain to tell to generations yet unborn the significant story. Amid the lavish plenty and solid freedom, and secure equity, and hospitable welcome to all men, it will stand to tell that by such men as you, under God's providence, such a goal was won. Your valor, your purpose, your endurance, your privations in camp and march, and field, your honorable wounds, the life devoted of your comrades were not in vain. The nation is one...Long after this memorial stone shall have crumbled, the generations to come will apprehend the results that came of this mighty struggle, in a united country, and a beneficent government, and a prosperous people.

God bless our whole land, and prosper it! And let all the people say, Amen!

In the years following the dedication ceremony, Reverend Thompson's health began to fail. He left Roosevelt Hospital and moved in with his daughter, Margaret Carpenter Hodenpyl, who was married to a diamond merchant. They had a comfortable home on Hobart Street in the affluent town of Summit, New Jersey. Thompson found great joy in his family and in his time of need, they tried to provide the same comfort he had given to thousands.

In 1894, at the age of seventy-two, Reverend Thompson became seriously ill. Although the nature of the illness wasn't recorded, "*for more than a year he suffered acute physical pain. But he kept his ministry until the New Year, and then strength failed. For six long weeks he faced death. His agony was constant.*" Despite the severe pain, Thompson's faith did not abandon him. He believed that "*there must be some reason. He knows, and I trust Him.*"

On the morning of February 7, 1895, Reverend Alexander Ramsay Thompson's suffering finally ended. On his coffin were inscribed the words, "*I shall be satisfied when I awake with Thy likeness.*" At his funeral, his children requested that the following hymn (which was written by Thompson and was his favorite) be read.

O blessed Lord, so well Thy work is done,
There is no need of its undoing; or
Of change of thought in Thee, the Holy One
Once done, forever done; what could be more!

And so, content am I, come what there may
From Thee to me; there can come never aught
But love has chosen it, and all my way,
Sunshine or shadow, is with blessing fraught.

Only such love as Thine would ever bear
Such weakness, folly, forwardness as mine;
And still, with gentle heavenly patience, care
For life like mine, enfolding it with Thine.

Darkened, bewildered though my way become
Chosen in love for me it is; what more
Have I the right to ask! it leads me home;
These are the steps up to my Father's door.

In the tradition of his family, Reverend Thompson had taken many steps in faithfully serving his country with the full measure of his devotion. More importantly, however, he took those steps of a rarer and more precious nature; those in the service to mankind.

Epilogue

An Unbroken Line

Alexander Ramsay Thompson, 1854-1922.

When Reverend Alexander Ramsay Thompson died in 1895, he was not the last in the line of patriotic Thompsons; indeed, the line continues through to today. The Reverend had at least two sons to carry on the tradition, William Robert Thompson, and yet another Alexander Ramsay Thompson (1854-1922). While Alexander chose the law as his profession, when the First World War began, like his father, he could not ignore his soldier's blood.

Despite being in his early sixties, Alexander donned a uniform and took "*great pleasure*" in serving his country with the Veteran Corps of Artillery, "*a military organization composed of lineal descendants of men who served in the Revolutionary War and the War of 1812*". While he did not see service overseas, his nephew, still another Alexander Ramsay Thompson (1895-1971) did, with the United States Navy.

Thompson family.

Both uncle and nephew served in World War I.

This younger Thompson would have two sons of his own who would serve their country; Alexander Ramsay Thompson, Jr. (1933-1995), who also served in the Navy,

Thompson family.

Alexander Ramsay Thompson (1933-1995) in the United States Navy in 1957, on board the U.S.S. Tanner off the coast of Turkey on a NATO mission.

and Robert Sands Thompson (1935-), who was in the Army. Robert Thompson also had two sons; another Robert Sands Thompson and still another Alexander Ramsay Thompson. While this youngest Alexander did not join the armed forces, he is an enthusiastic reenactor with a Confederate regiment in Virginia (What would the Reverend have thought?).

It is difficult to try to sum up in a few words, the lives of so many generations of Thompsons stretching the length of our nation's history. However, the memorial to the Alexander Ramsay Thompson who died in 1922, written by the Sons of the Revolution in the State of New York (of which he had been a founding member), comes close to encapsulating the spirit and essence of this brave and dedicated family. The six-page memorial states that during *the World War he worked in every available way for the success of the flag*. The document also describes this Thompson in words which no doubt could be used in regard to his father, granduncle and great-grandfather, as well as the Thompson women who shared the struggles of their men and country.

Cheerful and attractive in his manner, conservative in his advice and devoted in his loyalty...His patriotism and love of his country were deep seated and true...

The son of Reverend Thompson, Alexander R. Thompson, was a founding member of the Sons of the Revolution for the State of New York. The organization purchased and restored the historic Fraunces Tavern in lower Manhattan. This plaque, which is in the entranceway, bears his name.

150

Thompson family.

Four in a Row

Alexander Thompson (1933-1995) shakes the hand of his father, Alexander Thompson (1895-1971), on his wedding day, October 18,1962. Over the mantle, is the portrait of Captain Alexander Thompson (1759-1809). On the mantle, is the sword of Colonel Alexander Thompson (1793-1837) and his small, memorial portrait is hanging on the wall, just above the hilt.

Thompson family.

The most recent Alexander Ramsay Thompson (1972-) is a Civil War reenactor for a Confederate regiment, the 4th Alabama. (The Reverend Thompson would be pleased to know that on occassion, he is also a reenactor for the 79th New York.)

Bibliography

Adams, Henry. **The History of the United States During the Administration of Jefferson and Adams.** Chicago: University of Chicago Press, 1967.

Buckmaster, Henrietta. **The Seminole Wars.** New York: Collier Books, 1966.

Chartrand, Rene. **Uniforms and Equipment of the United States Forces in the War of 1812.** Youngstown, New York, 1992.

Colby, C. B. **Historic American Forts.** New York: Coward-McCann, 1963.

Cullum, Bvt. Major-General George. **Biographical Register of the Officers and Graduates of the United States Military Academy at West Point, New York.** New York: Houghton Mifflin & Company, 1891.

Dangerfield, George. **The Awakening of American Nationalism.** New York: Harper & Row, 1965.

Dunnigan, Brian Leigh & Scott, Patricia Kay. **Old Fort Niagara in Four Centuries.** Youngstown, New York: Old Fort Niagara Association, 1991.

Elkins, Stanley & McKitrick, Eric. **The Age of Federalism.** New York: Oxford University Press, 1993.

Ellis, David et al. **History of New York State.** Ithaca: Cornell University Press, 1967.

Esposito, Colonel Vincent, Ed. **The West Point Atlas of American Wars.** New York: Frederick Praeger, 1959.

Fast, Howard. **The Crossing.** New York: William Morrow & Company, 1971.

Fleming, Thomas. **West Point.** New York: William Morrow & Company, 1969.

Harper's Pictorial History of the Civil War. Chicago: Star Publishing, 1866.

Heinbach, Ellen & Kohlhagen, Gale. **West Point and the Hudson Valley.** New York: Hippocrene Books, 1990.

Heitman, Francis. **Historical Register and Dictionary of the United States Army.** Washington, D.C.: Government Printing Office, 1903.

Hickey, Donald. **The War of 1812.** University of Illinois Press, 1989.

LaBree, Benjamin, Ed. **The Pictorial Battles of the Civil War.** New York: Sherman Publishing, 1884.

Miller, Jeffrey. **The Federalist Era.** New York: Harper & Row, 1960.

Moat, Louis, Ed. **Famous Leaders and Battle Scenes of the Civil War.** New York: Leslie Publishing, 1896.

Orcutt, Reverend Samuel. **A History of the Old Town of Stratford and the City of Bridgeport.** Fairfield County: Fairfield County Historical Society, 1886.

Peterson, Harold. **The American Sword 1775-1945.** New Hope, PA: Robert Halter, 1954.

Porter, Phil. **The Eagle At Mackinac.** Mackinac Island, Michigan: Mackinac State Historic Parks, 1991.

Record of Service of the Connecticut Men. Hartford: Case Lockwood & Brainard Company, 1889.

Schachner, Nathan. **The Founding Fathers.** New York: Putnam, 1954.

Smelser, Marshall. **The Democratic Republic.** New York: Harper & Row, 1968.

Tomes, Dr. Robert. **Battles of America by Sea and Land.** New York: Patterson & Neilson, 1878.

The Story of the 21st Regiment of Connecticut Volunteers, by members of the Regiment. Middletown, Connecticut: Stewart Printing, 1900.

Weigley, Russell. **History of the United States Army.** New York: Macmillan, 1967.

Widder, Keith. **Reveille Till Taps.** Mackinac Island, Michigan: Mackinac State Historic Parks, 1994.

Index

Houston, General Sam, 80
Howe, Captain William, 111
Howe, Julia Ward, 139
Howell, Joseph, 6, 10
Hoyt, Captain Henry, 108, 111, 132, 143
Hubbard, Dr. Robert, 104, 113, 123, 125, 126
Hubbell, Captain William L., 108, 116, 123, 143
Hudson River, 9, 25, 50, 71
Hull, Franklin, 114
Hunztelman, Lt., 66
Hutchins, Lt., 13

—I—

Illinois, 71
Indiana, 71
Indiana Territory, 46
Ireland, 4, 15, 50
Iroquois Nation, 28
Irving, Washington, 4

—J—

Jackson, Andrew, 62, 64, 68, 82, 122
Jackson, General Stonewall, 108, 122
James River, 137
Jamieson, Lt., 74
Jay, Governor John, 24
Jefferson Barracks, 66
Jefferson, Thomas, 17, 23, 39, 40, 49, 52
Jenner, Edward, 38
Jesup, General, 81, 85
Jockey Hollow, New Jersey, 13
Jones, Brigadier General, 84

—K—

Kansas, 66, 75, 78
Kearny, Captain, 66, 68, 70
Key West, Florida, 114, 115
Knox, Henry, 7, 8, 9, 12, 13, 22, 24
Koehler, Carl, 138

—L—

La Baron, Dr. Francis, 46, 47
Lafayette, General, 23
Lake Champlain, 62, 63
Lake Erie, 41
Lake Huron, 46, 74
Lake Michigan, 46
Lake Ontario, 27, 41, 42
Lamb, Colonel John, 5
le Roe, Alfred, 120, 132
Lee, Henry "Light-Horse Harry", 61
Lee, Robert E., 61, 122, 127, 138
Liberia, 100
Lincoln, President Abraham, 105, 138
Lind, Jenny, 102

London, England, 102
Longstreet, General James, 133
Louis XVI, 22
Louisiana, 64, 66, 75, 78, 133, 144
Loyalists, 29

—M—

Macdonough, Master-Commandant Thomas, 63
Mackinac, 31, 46, 66, 71, 72, 73, 74, 95
Macomb, Major General Alexander, 62, 85
Macon, Georgia, 116
Madison Barracks, 68, 69
Madison, Connecticut, 132
Madison, New Jersey, 4
Madison, President James, 59
Maine, 71
Manassas, Virginia, 108, 112
Manhattan, 10, 13, 21, 22, 44, 68, 117, 150
Manville, Hiram, 133
Massachusetts, 138
McClallen, Lt., 13, 14, 20
McClellan House, Gettysburg, 144
McClellan, General George, 133
McKinley, Corporal George, 17, 18
Meade, General George, 127
Mexico, 80, 81, 93
Michigan, 95
Michigan Territory, 32, 38, 59, 71
Michilimackinac, 32, 45, 46, 47, 48, 62
Middletown, Connecticut, 16
Milledoler, Phillip, 67
Mississippi, 71
Mitchell, Mrs. M., 136-138
Mohawk River, 45
Monmouth, Battle of, 8
Montreal, Canada, 62, 74
Morris, Captain Staats, 17
Morristown, New Jersey, 10, 100
Mosby's Guerillas, 137

—N—

Napoleon, 60
Negro Fort, 82
New Amsterdam, 67
New England, 60, 71, 82, 117, 126
New England Soldiers' Relief Association, 117, 125, 134, 136, 138, 143
New Hampshire, 134
New Haven, Connecticut, 108, 143
New Orleans, Battle of, 64
New Orleans, Louisiana, 64, 133, 134
New York, 3, 4, 5, 6, 7, 8, 9, 10, 13, 15, 17, 18, 19, 20, 21, 22, 23, 24, 25, 26, 27, 29, 31, 37, 38, 39, 40, 41, 42, 44, 47, 50, 52, 54, 56, 59, 61, 67, 68, 69, 70, 71, 74, 75, 78, 83, 84, 85, 86, 89, 93, 99, 100, 105, 106, 115, 121, 122, 125, 126, 132, 134, 136, 139, 143, 150, 151

Swan, Caleb, 40, 41

Captain Thompson was with Colonel Lamb's Artillery during the Revolutionary War. The members of the Lamb's Artillery reenactment group are (from left to right), Carl Halgren, Cpl. Matt Koppinger, Douglas MacKinnon, Sgt. John Vilven, Richard Clair, John Medica, Lt. Al Florio and Joe Swain.

The gravestone of Captain Alexander Thompson and his wife, Amelia (center). The tall monument (left) marks the grave of their son, Lt. Col. Alexander Ramsay Thompson. The Colonel's wife, Mary, and his three sisters are buried next to him. These graves are in the United States Military Academy cemetery at West Point, New York, where Reverend Thompson paid his respects during a visit in 1861.

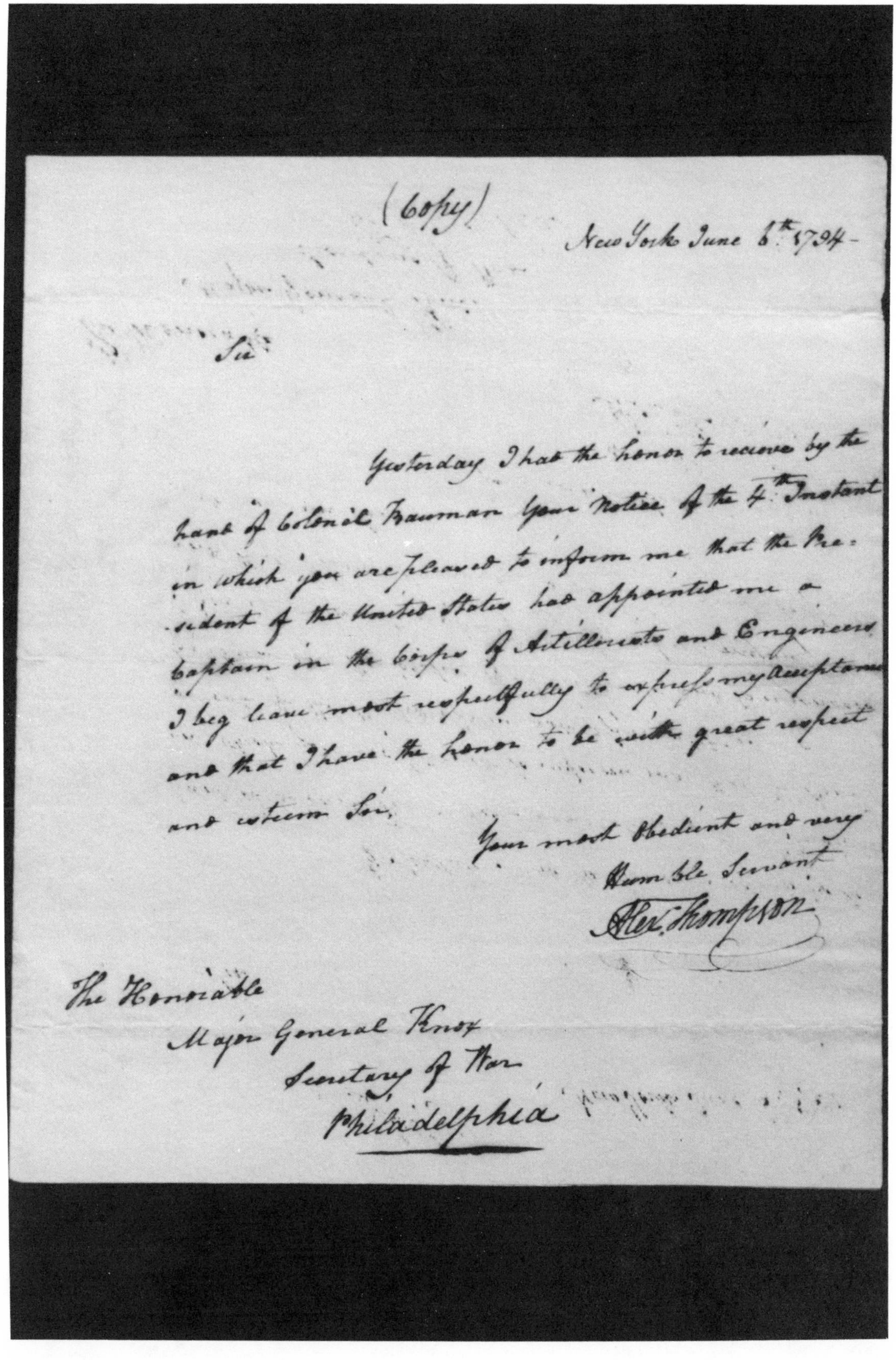

(Copy)
                                    New York June 6th 1794 –

Sir

        Yesterday I had the honor to receive by the
hand of Colonel Bauman your notice of the 4th Instant
in which you are pleased to inform me that the President of the United States had appointed me a
Captain in the Corps of Artillerists and Engineers
I beg leave most respectfully to express my Acceptance
and that I have the honor to be with great respect
and esteem Sir,
                        Your most Obedient and very
                                Hom ble Servant
                                Alex. Thompson

The Honorable
    Major General Knox
        Secretary of War
            Philadelphia

The letter from Alexander Thompson to Secretary of War Henry Knox, accepting his promotion to Captain of the Corps of Artillerists and Engineers.

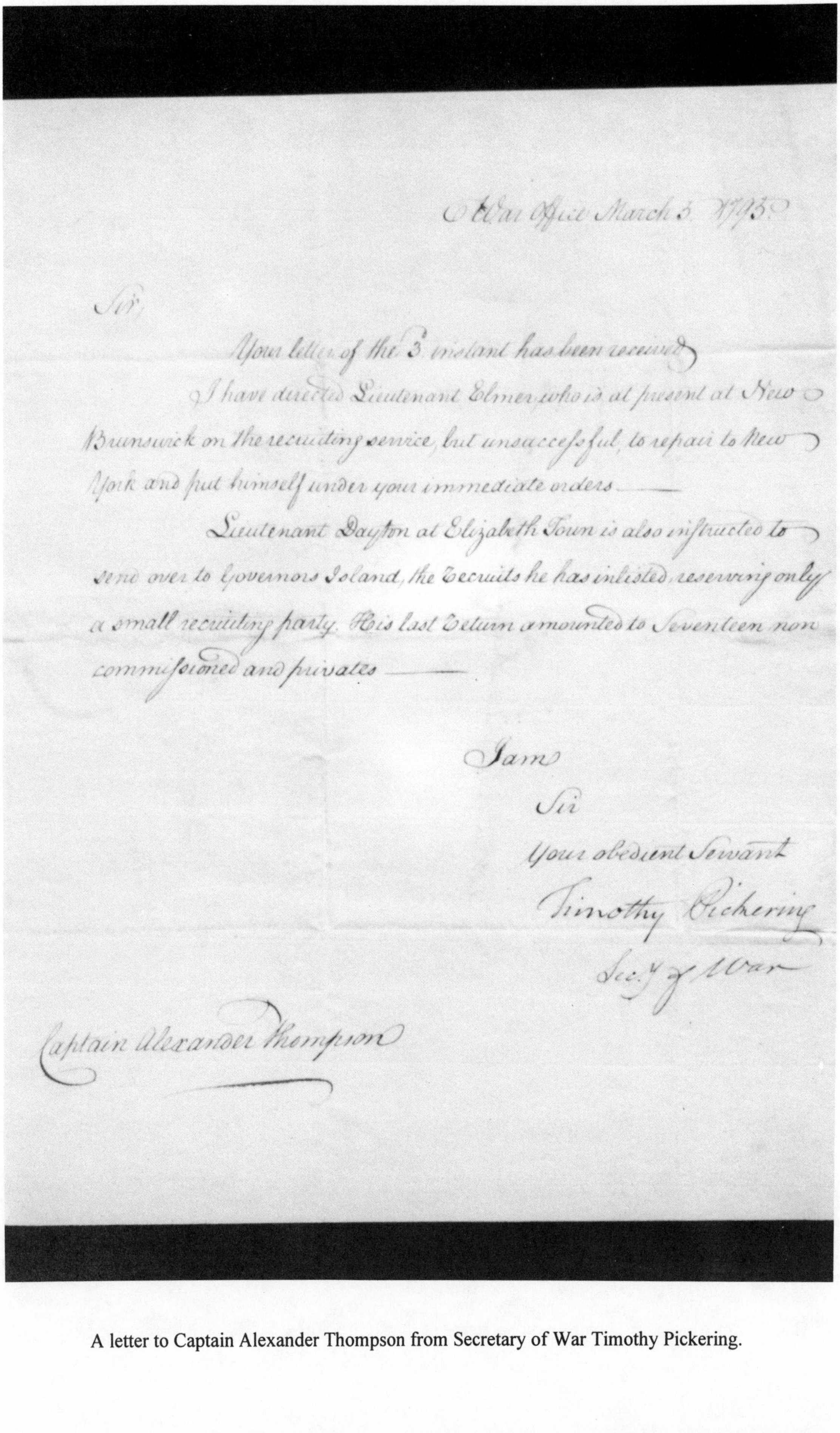

War Office March 5. 1795.

Sir,

Your letter of the 3. instant has been received.

I have directed Lieutenant Elmer who is at present at New Brunswick on the recruiting service, but unsuccessful, to repair to New York and put himself under your immediate orders. ———

Lieutenant Dayton at Elizabeth Town is also instructed to send over to Governors Island, the recruits he has inlisted reserving only a small recruiting party. His last Return amounted to Seventeen non commissioned and privates ———

I am
Sir
Your obedient Servant
Timothy Pickering
Sec.y of War

Captain Alexander Thompson

A letter to Captain Alexander Thompson from Secretary of War Timothy Pickering.

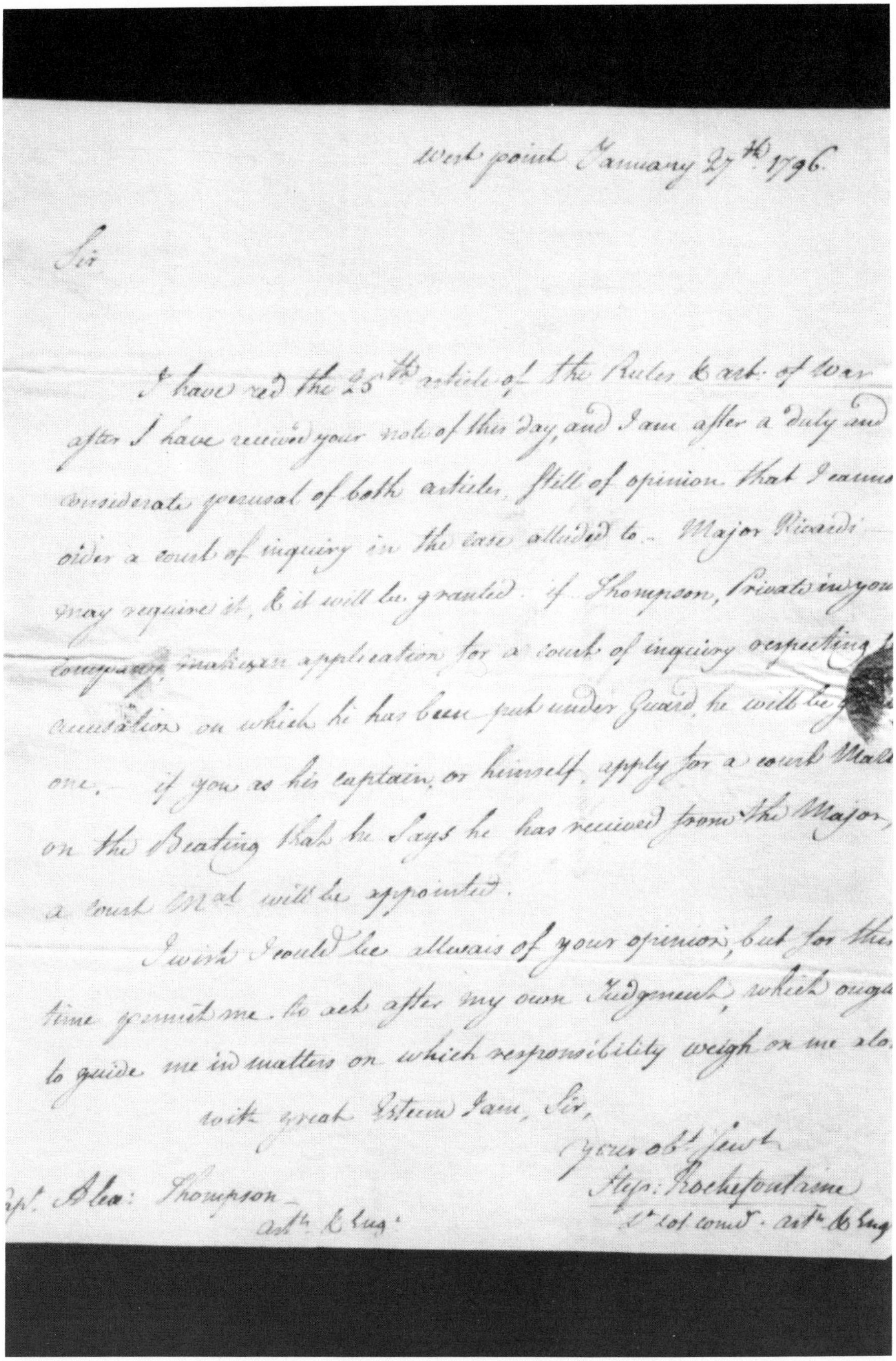

West point January 27th 1796

Sir

I have red the 25th article of the Rules & art: of war
after I have received your note of this day, and I am after a duly and
considerate perusal of both articles, still of opinion that I cannot
order a court of inquiry in the case alluded to. Major Rivardi
may require it, & it will be granted. if Thompson, Private in your
company makes an application for a court of inquiry respecting the
accusation on which he has been put under Guard, he will be granted
one. — if you as his captain, or himself, apply for a court Martial
on the Beating that he says he has received from the Major,
a court Martial will be appointed.

I wish I could be allways of your opinion, but for this
time permit me to act after my own Judgement, which ought
to guide me in matters on which responsibility weigh on me alone.

with great Esteem I am, Sir,

your obt. servt.
Steph: Rochefontaine
Lt col comd. art: & Eng:

Capt. Alex: Thompson
art: & Eng:

A letter from Lt. Col. Stephen Rochefontaine.

I James O'Ryan do solemnly swear to bear true allegiance to the United States of America, and to serve them honestly and faithfully against all their enemies or opposers whomsoever, and to observe and obey the orders of the President of the United States of America and the orders of the officers appointed over me, according to the articles of war ——

James O'Ryan

Sworn before me this
1st day of January 1799.

Enlistment papers.

The "Castle" at Fort Niagara (top). Canada is just across the river to the left. (Courtesy of Brian Dunnigan,
Old Fort Niagara.)
Front view of Fort Mackinac (bottom), looking out to the Straits of Mackinac. (Courtesy of Phil Porter,
Mackinac State Historic Parks.)

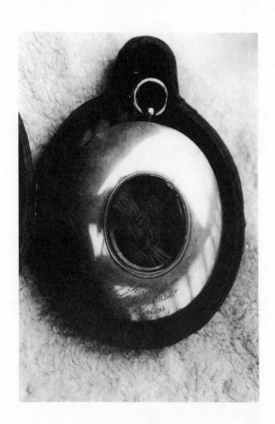

This miniature memorial portrait (approximately 3 inches in length) of Lt. Col. Thompson was painted on ivory, set in gold and fitted in a leather case. On the back, is a braided lock of his hair with the inscription:

Alex. R. Thompson
Lt. Col. 6th Reg. U.S. Inf.
Born Feb. 19th, 1793
Killed in Battle Dec. 25th, 1837

To the Honorable, the Senate, and House of Representatives of the United States, in Congress assembled.—

The Memorial of Mary W. Thompson

Widow of the late Lt Colonel Alexander Ramsay Thompson, of the United States Army, respectfully sheweth—

That having been placed by the Divine Providence, in a condition that renders it necessary for her to make application to Government for relief, she begs leave to present her case in such an aspect, as to exhibit the propriety and justice of her claim; and thereby induce your Honorable Body, so to favor it, that the result shall be, her obtaining the aid she thus so earnestly solicits.

My deceased lamented Husband, was the Son of the late Captain Alexander Thompson, of the United States Army, who was a Revolutionary Officer, having engaged in that service, at the age of sixteen years, and passed with Honor and Reputation through that memorable and sanguinary struggle, which gained for us as a Nation, Liberty and Independence.— His son, the late Lt Colonel Alexander R. Thompson, also entered the Service, as a Cadet at the Military Academy, West Point, in the year 1810, with a firm determination to devote his Life to the service and interests of his Country.

At the commencement of the war, in 1812, he was appointed a Lieutenant in the Army, and ordered to the North.— He was at the Siege of Plattsburgh, and tho' but a youth, in many instances Honorably distinguished himself.— in command of 100 men he gallantly defended a bridge, which the enemy was endeavouring to pass.— His Military skill and correct deportment, gained for him a character for science, intrepidity and cool deliberation (qualities which he truly possessed) and which bore him through the many trying situations in which he has been placed; and which he so affectingly exemplified in the disastrous Battle, wherein he generously and nobly yielded up his Life, in devotion to the interests of his Country—and to the honor of that Service, which was so closely interwoven with the best feelings of his heart.

Your Memorialist, would further most respectfully state, to the Honorable the Senate, and the House of Representatives, that my lamented Husbands Services, during the period of Twenty five years, have been unremitted.— He has served at every Military Post on the Northern Frontier—and on the Western, and South Western Border—He has planned and erected many of

Mary Thompson's plea to the government for a pension.

This fine portrait is of William Robert Thompson, the son of Captain Thompson, brother of Lt. Colonel Thompson and father of the Reverend Thompson. William owned a drugstore in Manhattan.

Monuments at Gettysburg National Military Park, dedicated to the 17th Connecticut Regiment of Volunteers. The monument on Barlow's Knoll (top) is at the scene of the first day's fighting. The monument on Cemetery Hill (bottom) was dedicated during a ceremony in which Reverend Thompson gave the oration in 1889.

This photograph, taken in Cheltenham, England, is of Matthew Agar, who came to America during the Civil War and enlisted with the 8th Regiment of New Hampshire Volunteers. Reverend Thompson was at Matthew's bedside when he died at the New England Soldiers' Relief Association in New York City and the Reverend wrote to Matthew's parents to tell them of his death. Mrs. Anne Agar sent this photo of her son to Reverend Thompson with a letter of thanks for his compassionate words.

Mine eyes have seen the glory of the coming of the Lord,
He is trampling out the vintage where the grapes of wrath
are stored;
He has loosed the fateful lightning of his terrible swift sword,
His truth is marching on.
Chorus Glory Glory Hallelujah &c

I have seen him in the watch fires of an hundred circling camps,
They have builded him an altar in the evening dews and damps,
I have read his righteous sentence by the dim and flaring lamps,
Our God is marching on.

I have read his fiery gospel writ in burnished lines of steel;
As ye deal with my contemners so my grace with you shall deal;
Let the hero born of woman crush the serpent with his heel,
Since God is marching on.

He has sounded forth the trumpet which shall never call retreat;
He is sifting out the hearts of men before his judgment seat;
Oh be swift my feet to answer him! be jubilant my feet!
As God is marching on.

In the beauty of the lilies, Christ was born across the sea,
With a glory in his bosom which transfigures you and me;
As he died to make men holy, let us die to make men free
Since God is marching on.

Copied on steamship "United States" off "Tortugas" where
are confined the assassins of the murderer of his country
September 27th 1865
Charles F Foster

The Thompson family, circa 1890. The Reverend Thompson is standing (center) smoking a pipe. His wife, Mary, is seated to his right.

To order <u>autographed</u> copies of

<u>From Revolution to Civil War</u>

Please send a check or money order for $24.95 for each copy (shipping & handling included) to:

Eagle Press
P.O. Box 487
Piermont, New York
10968

Name_____

Address_____

_____

City_____ **State**_____ **Zip**_____

Eagle Press, P.O. Box 487, Piermont, New York, 10968

To order __autographed__ copies of

From Revolution to Civil War

Please send a check or money order for $24.95 for each copy (shipping & handling included) to:

Eagle Press
P.O. Box 487
Piermont, New York
10968

Name_____

Address_____

_____

City_____ **State**_____ **Zip**_____

Eagle Press, P.O. Box 487, Piermont, New York, 10968

About the Author

Since childhood, Linda Zimmermann has had many interests and regretted only being able to major in two subjects in college; chemistry and English literature. While working as a Research Scientist during the 1980's, she decided to continue her education, received a Master of English degree and soon realized that writing was becoming more than just an enjoyable pastime.

Trading her test tubes for a word processor, Linda has spent the last several years as a freelance writer. Among her publications, are articles on science, medicine, ancient history, American history and religion, as well as works of short fiction. She has appeared on television and radio, teaches and lectures frequently. In addition, she exhibits her "Spacescapes"; oil paintings of planets, nebulas and galaxies.

Linda's first book, *Bad Astronomy* (published 1995), traces the history of unusual astronomical theories from the ancient Greeks to the present. The book, which critics called "*a wonderful resource...fascinating, fact-filled and amusing*", has sold throughout the United States, Canada, Europe, Japan and Australia.

Forging A Nation, her second book, afforded Linda the opportunity of combining her love of research and history with her unique storytelling ability. It was a project in which she became completely immersed; a condition she confesses is not uncommon in her work or numerous hobbies.

To take a break from the keyboard, Linda takes long walks and hikes with her three dogs; a husky named Andromeda and two German shepherds, Orion and Sid. She also enjoys tennis, opera, old movies, cooking and collecting "just about everything".

*The author would appreciate learning any new information
concerning the Thompson family and the whereabouts of
any related documents or artifacts. Please write to:*

Linda Zimmermann
C/O Eagle Press
P.O. Box 487
Piermont, New York
10968